Social Disorganization
in America

Chandler Publications in Anthropology and Sociology

LEONARD BROOM, Editor

PUBLIC LEADERSHIP
Wendell Bell, Richard J. Hill, Charles R. Wright

THE ARCHAEOLOGIST'S NOTE BOOK
Clement W. Meighan

AN INTRODUCTION TO INDUSTRIAL
  SOCIOLOGY
Charles B. Spaulding

FORMAL ORGANIZATIONS
Peter M. Blau and W. Richard Scott

SOCIAL DISORGANIZATION IN AMERICA
Reece McGee

SOCIAL

DISORGANIZATION

IN

AMERICA

by REECE McGEE
The University of Texas

CHANDLER PUBLISHING COMPANY
San Francisco

This book is dedicated, with respect and with love

to

Mrs. Margaret Carroll
Mrs. Myrtle Dale
Miss Alice Grendall
Miss Blanche Kelly
Miss Jane Kennedy
Miss Audrey Lloyd
Miss Lucille Lyons
Miss Constantia Mohr
Mrs. Marion Boggs Moscrip
Miss Ella Roverud

sometime teachers or principals of the Richards Gordon School of St. Paul, Minnesota, and to the thousands of devoted men and women who give their lives to the instruction of elementary-school children.

The infantry in man's unending battle with ignorance, their works and their sacrifices are often forgotten and ever unsung.

PREFACE

This book deals with the phenomenon sociologists call "social disorganization." Since you have elected to read it, or to take a course in which its reading is required, it is not unfair to assume that you have some idea of what the term stands for. Indeed when students in classes with the same title are asked to give examples of social disorganization, their responses are predictable: war, crime, juvenile delinquency, promiscuity, drug addiction, alcoholism, suicide, divorce, etc., all occur with considerable regularity. This is hardly surprising and most texts in the subject have such topics as their chapter titles or section-headings. But if the reader will consider the range of phenomena included under these topics in all their variations and disparity, he will conclude that the term "social disorganization" includes a variety of dissimilar behaviors. As a matter of fact, the sociological study of social disorganization is at best greatly confused, and at worst, anarchic. The title covers a host of social ills, problems, departures from idiosyncratic ethical standards, and the like. The very disparity of the topics included in the list above is an indication of the confusion now reigning. The purpose of this work is to try to bring some system to the study of social disorganization.

At the outset the student should be clear that identification of any given state of affairs as "disorganized" necessarily implies the existence (in the mind of the identifier) of some conception of what constitutes "organization." Further, there is a value-assumption about what is "organized" in the identification of any state of affairs as "disorganized." This value-loading is implicit in any "social-problems" approach to the field because a situation is only problematic relative to some human point of view or ethical standard. But one man's meat is another man's poison, and while divorce may be a problem from an ethical-religious point of view, it is hardly problematic to the Las Vegas lawyer who specializes in handling divorce actions. It is the "social-problems" approach which, as a result of its evaluative character, introduces the confusion noted above into the study of social disorganization.

This work attempts a nonevaluative theoretical approach. The formulation on which it is based and which is illustrated throughout is outlined by Arnold Rose in his essay, "A Theory of Social Organization and Disorganization." [1] Rose's treatment of the subject matter is particularly valuable in summing up a great deal of sociological thought and in presenting in propositional form a sociological theory holding that disorganization consists in deviation from social norms. In this view a *social problem* (such as divorce or juvenile delinquency) is a set of behaviors which are the result of contradictions or conflicts within a normative system or the result of the absence of a normative system covering the specific behaviors in question. This condition of conflict within norms or lack of norms concerning behavior is social disorganization.

The major theoretical stumbling block of the more usual "social-problems" approach to the subject is that a given behavior, for example delinquency, is first defined as a social problem and then investigated in order to determine its own causes. Theoretically the social problem is treated both as a cause and as an effect. Fuller and Myers criticized the "social-problems" viewpoint in 1941, noting that it often led to the presentation of undigested and unsystematic masses of data about crime, divorce, insanity, and the like.[2] In a later article the same authors further clarify the concept of the social problem. "In the last analysis, social problems arise and are sustained because people do not share the same common values and objectives." [3]

[1] Arnold Rose, *Theory and Method in the Social Sciences* (Minneapolis: University of Minnesota Press, 1954), pp. 3-24.

[2] Richard C. Fuller and Richard R. Myers, "Some Aspects of a Theory of Social Problems," *American Sociological Review*, 6:1, February, 1941.

[3] Richard C. Fuller and Richard R. Myers, "The Natural History of a Social Problem," *American Sociological Review*, 6:3, June, 1941, p. 32.

Rose's formulation of this approach and its application to specific problem situations in this book expands the foregoing statement and may be summarized under the following three propositions which should be considered a kind of "thumbnail outline" of the theory.

AN OUTLINE OF SOCIAL DISORGANIZATION

1. Most people do (pretty much) what is expected of them.
2. When an individual or a group fails to do what is expected in a social system, social disorganization has occurred.
3. This social disorganization results from either or both of the following conditions:

    a. The absence of a recognized set of expectations for behavior.
    b. Contradictions or incompatibilities within the recognized set of expectations for behavior.

Beware the apparent simplicity of these propositions; their implications extend deeply into the major subject areas of sociology, explaining or affecting much of socialization, social psychology, collective behavior, social organization, and social control.

ACKNOWLEDGMENTS

Many persons are responsible for the production of a book; often the author acts only as the literary focus of an ambience of other writers, publishers, editors, critics, students, and assistants, and it is possible for him to acknowledge by name only the small number of them who gave him specific assistances. The others, who may be responsible for many of the ideas which fill his pages and which he has made his own, must remain anonymous.

I must gratefully acknowledge the assistance of the many publishers and authors who gave me permission to use portions from or adaptations of their copyrighted works for which specific citations will be found on the pages where those works appear. I am further indebted to Leonard Broom to whose editorial counsel the book owes much of what clarity it has; to Professor George Vold of The University of Minnesota for permission to use his thoughts on the sociology of conflict; to the Hogg Foundation for Mental Hygiene of The University of Texas for funds which helped support secretarial assistance, and to Mrs. Margaret V. Wheeler for that immensely useful assistance. Finally I am also deeply grateful to the hundreds of students in my classes who have been exposed to, commented upon, criticized, and corrected the ideas contained herein, and by their enthusiasm for them given me the initiative to put them down.

RM^c

The University of Texas
July, 1961

CONTENTS

Social Disorganization
in America

Chapter I

SOME ASPECTS OF SOCIAL PSYCHOLOGY

Introduction

An understanding of the theory of social organization and disorganization is furthered by comprehension of Meadian social psychology. While the fundamental concepts of the social behaviorist approach are probably familiar to most readers, we will restate them shortly for the sake of familiarity and specific applicability.

MEAD'S SOCIAL PSYCHOLOGY[1]

The social psychology of George Herbert Mead, sometimes called Social Behaviorism or Symbolic Interactionism, amends some of the theoretical weaknesses of Cooley's earlier formulations.[2] Cooley had postulated the inseparability of the individual and society. To use the illustration of a coin: A coin to be a *coin* must have two faces, a head and a tail. It is possible upon occasion for a "coin" to have either two heads or two tails, for the mints do make mistakes. But when this happens the coin in question is not really a coin; it is a disk of metal with embossing on it; it is not a valid coin. In the same way, the individual and his society are two sides of the same coin. A personality is not a personality without both sides, and to speak of it as consisting of one side without

[1] This section follows closely the discussion in Don Martindale and Elio D. Monachesi, *Elements of Sociology* (New York: Harper and Brothers, Publishers, 1951), pp. 296-299, copyright Harper and Brothers, 1951. Published with the permission of the authors and the publisher.

[2] See Charles H. Cooley, *Human Nature and the Social Order* (New York: Charles Scribner's Sons, 1902), especially Chapter III.

●   3   ●

reference to the other would be as meaningless as to describe a "coin" as consisting of only one face. But Cooley regarded society simply as a community of ideas existing in the mind of the individual. Mead focuses on the social behavior of individuals rather than their psychology; upon what people *do* rather than how they *think*. With this shift, the problem becomes not, as it was for Cooley, how individual experience contributes to the creation of the personal idea, but rather how that idea and the human personality ultimately develop out of social actions. The central focus of his analysis is on *language*.

The Significance of Language in the Development of Personality

Mead maintains that the specific mechanism which everywhere precedes the development of language or communication proper is the gesture. Even among animals, when interactions occur, gestures are frequently a part of them. Mead defines a gesture as any phase of a social act or interaction which comes to be used as a *sign* for those phases yet to occur. He illustrates this point with the example of a dog fight.

Imagine two dogs, strangers to each other, who round the corner of a brick building on a city sidewalk and suddenly find themselves nose to nose. What is likely to be the outcome of this situation? Perhaps one of the two might fall into a defensive posture: forelegs stiffened, hind legs crouched, hackles rising, teeth bared, low rumbling growl in the throat, and associated attitudes. Let us call this dog, Dog One. Dog Two, equally surprised at this unexpected encounter, sees Dog One fall into this posture from which an attack may be made. Dog Two might interpret this behavior ("say to himself," as it were) as preparation for attack. He, then, believing that Dog One was about to attack him, would fall into a similar defensive position. But the problem is that Dog One, seeing Dog Two fall into this defensive posture, "thinks to himself" that his initial defense reaction was correct, for is not Dog Two now indeed preparing to attack him? And so the encounter eventuates in the swirling whirlpool of yelps and fur that we recognize as a dog fight. Mead has this to say about it:[3]

I have given the illustration of the dog fight as a means of presenting the gesture. The act of each dog becomes the stimulus of the other dog for his response. There is, thus, a relationship between the two; and as the act is responded to by the other dog, it, in turn, undergoes change. The very fact that the dog is ready to attack another becomes a stimulus to the other dog to change his own position or his own attitude. He has no sooner done this than the change of attitude in the second dog in turn causes the first dog to change his attitude. We have here a conversation of gestures.

But gestures are not words and a "conversation of gestures" of this nature cannot truthfully be called communication. The significant point about the animal interaction just described is that the gestures of each animal mean to the other things different from what they mean or are "intended" to mean by the dog making them. Each dog "thinks" that he is preparing to defend himself from a presumed attack by the other. Because of the inability of the two to understand the proper significance of the gestures formed by their postures, a combat unintended by either ensues. It is, thus, only when a gesture of some kind has the same meaning for both parties to an interaction that it becomes a *significant symbol*.

Recall that Mead defines the gesture as a *sign* standing for phases of an act yet to come. The distinctions between sign, symbol, and significant symbol are crucial.

The *sign* relationship may be thought of as one where the events in the relationship are somehow *naturally* associated with each other, the structuring of the association being unaffected by the uses of man. For example, smoke is a *sign*

[3] G. H. Mead, *Mind, Self, and Society* (Chicago: University of Chicago Press, 1934), pp. 42-43. Copyright 1934 by The University of Chicago. Published with the permission of the University of Chicago Press.

of fire, and dark clouds a *sign* of rain. We perceive that the events are associated in nature.

The *symbol* relationship is one wherein the events related are associated with each other arbitrarily, as a deliberate act of human invention. Man is a symbol-using animal and we live in a symbolic world, surrounded at all times by thousands upon thousands of symbols and symbol relationships. Let us take for illustration the very common symbol of the red light. What kinds of events does this artifact symbolize? It would be impossible, of course, to list every possible meaning of this symbol, but a compilation of the categories of events for which the red light is symbolic might include, minimally, the following:

1. House of prostitution.

2. Mechanical malfunction (as in automobiles to symbolize the failure of oil pressure, of electric generation, to release a handbrake; in more complex machinery to symbolize circuit failure, fire, interruption of operation).

3. Halt forward motion (the stop sign).

4. Danger: (a) Of obstruction in right of way normally unobstructed (as symbolized by the red lantern or the flare before the hole in the street, the flashing red light at a railroad crossing to indicate the passage of a train, the flare or reflector put out on the highway by the driver of a heavy truck parked on the shoulder). (b) Of permanent obstacles (such as radio broadcasting towers, traffic islands in highways, support pillars of bridges or overpasses).

5. Exit.

6. Navigational direction signals (on aircraft or ships marking the port wing or side).

7. Emergency vehicle demanding right of way (as on police cars, ambulances, fire trucks).

Since the steady or flashing red light is used to symbolize all of these quite different things, it is evident that the *meaning* of the red light is not *in* any of these things, but is rather assigned to them by the context in which they occur. There is nothing about the intrinsic nature of a red light which must stand for or symbolize any of these things. The attachment of the red light to the meaning symbolized is arbitrary; the light could as well be blue, pink, or lime green. The meaning is assigned by the men who use the symbol, it is not "given" in the relationship itself. But the relationship between the red light and any of the meanings above is one which must be learned. A symbol the meaning of which is unknown has no significance for the individual. A motorist who has never seen a stop light will not be aware that a red light means he should stop.

A symbol becomes *significant* only when the meaning assigned to it is known to the individual who perceives it. An excellent and familiar example is that of the symbol system we call musical notation. To an individual who does not read music the printed page of notes and bars has little or no meaning. He may recognize it as a printed page of music, but if it is untitled he is unable to tell a Bach fugue from rock-and-roll. The notes and bars are simply print on a page, chicken tracks, to him. To the conductor of a symphony orchestra, however, the printed symbols have such meaning that, just in reading them, he is likely to be able to hear the music in his mind, to invest such meaning in the symbols that he can create in his own imagination the sounds for which the symbols stand. For him, the symbols are significant.

In the case of the dog fight, one can see a series of gestures initiated by each animal which arouse in the other more or less appropriate responses. In the case of a significant symbol system, a red light or a musical score, there is a symbol which has a meaning in the experience of the first party to the interaction (the man who designed the traffic light, or the composer of the score), and which calls forth that same meaning in the experience of the second party to the interaction (the motorist approaching the signal or the conductor reading the score). The symbol, in other words, has attained significance, and at this point true communication has occurred.

Just as the meaning of a gesture, in Mead's definition, lies in the phases of the interaction that have yet to occur, so does the meaning of a significant symbol also lie in the future course of a social act. According to Mead the meaning of a symbol for an individual lies in his tendency to respond to it. He uses the illustration of a student asked by his instructor to bring a chair for a visitor to the classroom. The student is likely to fulfill the request, but if he does not the instructor will probably do so himself, for in the act of asking the student to secure the chair he has stimulated *himself* to do so, provided a stimulus for his own response. It is exactly at this point that the major difference between human and animal behavior is apparent. Through the use of significant symbols, one man arouses the same tendencies in himself that he does in the other, and in doing so he puts himself in the place of the other. Before one person can initiate any action in another person by the provision of an appropriate symbol for him, the initiating individual must first, in a sense, say to himself, "If I want to produce such and such a response in this person, what will it take to do it? What would it take to make me act in this way?" Then, having selected the symbol that would elicit the desired response in himself, the initiator proceeds to suggest the symbol to the other. In this way the use of the significant symbol demands a sharing of experiences, and, since the same tendencies created by or stimulated through the use of the symbol are aroused in both the initiator and the receiver of it, the action is *shared*. In this way the *meaning* of a symbol is something objectively present as a relationship between certain phases of a social act. The meaning of a symbol lies in the commonly shared experiences which all parties to the symbol relationship possess. Human experiences being, for the large part, typical and repeatable, meanings in many cases become nearly universal.

THE SELF

The word "self" does not refer to a corporeal body. The "self," though it obviously includes the body, usually refers to something else as well. The body is an object or a possession of the thing referred to by the self symbols: "my arms" or "my head" are the arms or the head which belong to the entity which is "me," "my self." The self has the unique characteristic that of all of the events in the universe it is the only one which can be an object to itself. Only a self can examine itself, can, as an active agent or subject, examine its own actions in a predicative or objective sense. In this way the self can be both subject and object simultaneously, and this characteristic differentiates it from all other events. The significance of language is apparent here, for language—a system of significant symbols—is the only form of behavior which permits an organism to become an object to itself. The whole process is evidenced in the way in which a child acquires his language.

A small child must (because of his tremendous dependence upon her), conform to his mother's ways of doing things and her ideas of propriety and probity. Mothers are usually determined to raise their children properly. This determination operates on both conscious and unconscious levels, for, while the mother may sometimes rationally and self-consciously teach the child to behave in certain ways in order that his skills may reflect credit upon herself, she enforces the majority of her rules for his behavior without being aware that they are rules at all, and she enforces them not because things "ought" to be done that way, but rather because it never occurs to her that there are alternatives. How many American mothers consider, for example, that one possible occupation for their offspring is that of pauper? How many American parents raise their children to be failures? The aspiration for success, part of the propriety of American living, is seldom engendered in the child self-consciously through specific teaching; rather it is simply part of the way the world works, like the setting of the sun, and the mother—the unconscious agent of cultural transmission—teaches the child to value success without even knowing that she is doing so.

In these ways ideas of propriety are engendered. The mother in effect assumes the attitudes of her society toward the baby and insists that he conform to them. She may be likened to a lens which focuses the diffuse rules of her culture, both acknowledged and implied, upon the child. In the first years of a baby's life, she and his father (and older

9

siblings if there are any) are the only agents of his society with which he has any contact. Since these agents have internalized the rules and the values and the definitions by which their society operates, the infant learns them as a matter of course through their insistence upon his conforming to "their" ideas. In this insistence the mother employs some kind of simplified language—baby talk—to the child. Take, for example, "no-no", a symbol frequently heard by infants between 12 and 24 months of age. "No-no" is applied to all things prohibited to him—touching a hot iron, pulling the cat's tail, throwing his oatmeal on the floor, playing in that most fascinating of objects, the toilet. The meaning of the word "no" is *in* all of these acts. The child soon learns that the word, which at first is only a sign to him, stands for the concept of prohibition. "No-no" means that he must stop, or withdraw, or ignore a variety of events and objects and situations.

But in acquiring the meaning of the term, the baby also acquires the attitudes associated with the behaviors in question. When his mother, busy at her ironing, sees him reach for the shiny iron, and says "no-no" she is apt to say it with emotional overtones and loadings in her voice which scream "danger" at him, which express concern and the immediacy of anxiety. When she hears the yowling of the cat and enters the room to find the baby swinging the animal around his head by the tail, and tells him, "No-no, poor pussy, no-no," the emotional nuances of her voice express sympathy with the animal and affection for it, and perhaps reproof for the baby's act of thoughtless cruelty. When, on the other hand, she becomes aware of a silence of some minutes' duration (the danger signal of toddlerhood) and searches for the child to find him happily playing with the contents of an unflushed toilet, she says, "No-no, uugghh! dirty, nasty, mustn't touch, ooooo!" And under these circumstances what the infant hears is revulsion and loathing, and he is likely to carry this attitude toward excrement for the remainder of his life. (Note here, that tiny infants and animals do not find the odor or consistency, or even taste, of excrement offensive. Apparently its repulsive quality is learned.)

The word "no-no" thus becomes a symbol for each of these acts, and the acts themselves become associated in the child's mind with the emotions his mother has manifested when she used the symbol in context with them. In time the child comes to use the same verbal symbol for the act that his mother uses to him, and when he does he arouses in himself the same attitude toward these acts that his mother aroused in him in the past through her use of the symbol. It is not uncommon, for example, to see a toddler of perhaps eighteen months standing in front of some forbidden object like the television set, reaching out with one chubby hand toward the dial and then slapping the offending hand with the other, and saying, "No-no, bad boy, mustn't touch." What the child is doing at this point, of course, is stimulating himself by his act of reaching to initiate an appropriate response, in this case the prohibitory symbol and action of his mother, the same behaviors he has elicited from her in the past by his act of reaching. The child is taking the role of the mother and acting toward himself in the way in which she has acted toward him in the past. Thus, through use, through the infant's taking the role of the mother, the word "no-no" ceases to be a sign and becomes a significant symbol. The standpoint of the other is thus implicit in every significant symbol. In order to use the symbol at all one must share its meaning with others and this sharing implies mutual role taking.

THE SIGNIFICANCE OF PLAY
IN PERSONALITY DEVELOPMENT

"Play" has a variable meaning; it is not the same at all ages, the play of a two-year-old being quite different from that of a five-year-old. The play of small children often appears to be supportive of their thought processes. As the child's verbal ability increases with advancing age, his play takes increasingly organized forms, and he begins to take play roles. Anyone who has observed small children knows how complex this role-taking can become, with fairly complicated social situations being reproduced. The roles of play are sometimes executed in detail and with extravagant imagination. For example, the little girl having a tea party with her animals and dolls lays her tiny table with her doll dishes and puts a doll or a stuffed animal at each place, and then, acting the role of gracious hostess, picks up her teapot full of water and solicitously asks the teddy bear if he would have some tea. Then, putting down the teapot, she shifts her stance and walks around the table to stand behind the teddy bear, answering the question she has just asked in a high squeaky voice and replying that indeed she (the teddy bear) would like some. This shift of speaking voice is projected to each doll or animal in the play, and serves to mark off the limits of the different roles for her; the physical shifting of positions makes the roles more distinct.

The Game and the Generalized Other

The game, as distinct from free play, introduces a new level of personality organization in the child. In play each role is relatively independent. The child may make up the story as he goes along, shifting characters and moods, and his playmates, because of the freedom of their own responses to his actions, are able to keep up with him. The roles in a game, however, are of a different order. For in the game each role is intimately related to every other and derives its meaning from them. For example, in hide-and-seek there are but two roles: the hider and the seeker, and yet to see the intimacy with which these roles are related one has only to consider the meaninglessness of hiding if no one seeks, or the meaninglessness of seeking if no one hides. (Many of us can remember the game of hide-and-seek where our playmates made us "it." After counting two hundred with eyes buried in forearms, we sought the hiders for some time before it dawned upon us that they had fled. The confusion and hurt and sense of loss in the individual who discovers that he is playing a group game alone illustrates the total relevancy and interdependence of roles in the game.)

In hide-and-seek the role of seeker has meaning only with relation to that of hider, and vice versa. In more complicated games, such as baseball, the roles of each player are not only dependent for their meaning upon those of every other player and the performance of individuals in those roles, but also upon the behavior of the members of the opposing team, for teams play as wholes in games, and the response of every player to every other is organized in terms of definite rules for the behaviors of the individual members of these wholes. The transition from the fluid role-taking of play to the more complex role-taking of the game is hardly simple. The attitude (or role) the child takes in play is that of a particular other person: the cowboy, the teddy bear, the mother, the policeman. The attitude he must take to play the game, however, is of an entirely different kind for it involves taking the roles, sharing the viewpoints, of not just a particular other individual but a number of others: the members of both teams.

This situation, where it is demanded that the individual simultaneously take the roles (points of view) of a number of other individuals and in which the role-taking is organized according to specific rules, is similar to the situation of the individual in the social group or community. It is the social group which gives unity of self to the human individual. This group may be called The Generalized Other. The Generalized Other is the impersonal "they" to which we refer, the people of "what will 'they' think?" or "what will 'people' think?"— the impersonal, faceless, anonymous "they" to which all of us refer many of our behaviors.

In the course of a human life this impersonal "they"— society—expects many different things from the individual. His parents may want him to be quiet and studious and obedient, but—if he is a boy—his play group may accept him only if he is loud and audacious and lazy and dirty. In this contradictory way each role that he plays throughout life competes for him and for his time and attention with every other role. Each makes demands in the form of expectations for his

• 13

behavior. But the personality cannot be adequately described simply as a collection of roles the individual takes, for some roles have major significance while others have very little, and, further, integrations occur continuously which eliminate some roles, add others, and modify yet others. The selection of a mate or the choice of an occupation are major integrations of this kind. Once the integrations are made, a number of other roles formerly played fall into disuse and new roles are called for.

And "they" do something else as well; not only do "they" have numbers of differing expectations for the behavior of the individual, but "they" also make judgments about his performance in these roles. To be sure, the performance of some roles is subject to extremely wide variation, but in most of them both technical and ethical judgments are made with regard to the adequacy of the individual's fulfillment of expectation.

This discussion underscores the thoroughly learned and entirely social nature of much of the human personality and all of its social behavior. Thought, and those most intimate of all subjective phenomena, conceptions of self, take place in terms learned from and in interaction with others. This interaction continually goes on (for personality is not static, but is constantly modified) in the process of fulfilling the expectations of others for one's behavior. These expectations are not always those of specific others with whom one has relatively intimate relationships; often they issue not from individuals at all but rather from the more impersonal contexts of social groups and organizations.

Social Organization[4]

Like other scientific concepts, sociological ideas get their significance from the phenomena to which they refer

[4] This discussion follows closely that in Don Martindale and Elio D. Monachesi, *Elements of Sociology* (New York: Harper and Brothers, 1951), pp. 382-384. Copyright Harper and Brothers, 1951. Used with the permission of the authors and publisher.

in the real world. It is useful now to discuss the ideas and phenomena termed "events," "institutions," and "organizations" or "associations."

The objects of scientific observation are usually called "events." A physicist may investigate such events as balls rolling down inclined planes, and pendulums swinging. When he investigates them his interest does not lie in any single event, a red ball rolling down a particular inclined plane, nor in a single class of events, such as pendulums swaying. His interest lies in the fact that these events, rolling balls and swinging pendulums, are members of a general class of events called falling bodies. Nor is the scientist interested in the intrinsic qualities of the events themselves. It matters not whether the balls are red or green and it makes no difference whether the pendulum hangs from a grandfather clock or a carpenter's plumb line. The interest of the scientist is in how these events occur and he aspires to give a general formulation to their occurrence. Thus when the velocity of falling bodies is expressed in the formula $\frac{1}{2} gt^2$ (one-half of gravity times time squared) the problem of general formulation is solved. This familiar example from high-school science courses is equivalent to the ways in which the concepts of sociology are developed. The objects of any scientific investigation are called "events" and the objects of sociological investigation are "social events."

The most fundamental kind of events the sociologist investigates are called social actions, actions oriented either directly or indirectly to other people, the things that people do to or for or with reference to one another as well as *with* one another. Not all human behavior consists of social actions. Eating, sleeping, and other biological phenomena are not social actions. What one eats and what one eats it with and how often and where and with whom, are all determined socially and are, therefore, social actions. These social events are just as objective—as *real*—as falling bodies or swinging pendulums. Eating with a fork is real. Holding a preference for sleeping with one's head on a wooden block is equally real.

When a scientist discerns a number of events occurring

together and seeming to have similar kinds of consequences he may view the whole pattern of these events as what is called a complex event. One such event often investigated by early chemists (and today in secondary-school science classes) is the solution of salt in water and its recrystallization out of solution at the saturation point. In the same way a complicated series of social actions which recur with regularity over time may be regarded as a complex event by a sociologist. A *social group is one such event*, a specific concrete entity. A group is distinguished here from a mere collectivity or aggregation. The assortment of people that collects at the head of the stairs in your class building between classes is not a group. It is a crowd or collectivity or aggregate. A group has the particular characteristics that it endures over time and that its members tend to behave in regular and predictable ways toward one another. The enduring character of the complex social event called a group arises out of the fact that the members of the group act in particular ways toward one another, that they have expectations for each others' behaviors, and that these expectations tend generally to be fulfilled. A social group, thus, is a complex, organized unit of social action.

The term "institution" is another one commonly used in sociology. Social institutions are patterns or rules for behavior, many of them unformulated and, indeed, even unarticulated by the individuals who follow them. These patterns or rules for relationships which hold within and between social groups define the actions of those groups. Social institutions, then, are some of the $\frac{1}{2} gt^2$ of sociology. $\frac{1}{2} gt^2$ is not a falling body but rather is a rule or description of the pattern in which bodies fall. The American family institution, similarly, is not *a* family; it is the rules or patterns of relationships which define the ways in which American families and their members behave.

A third term with which the student should be familiar is "organization," sometimes called "association." This term refers to collections of social groups organized according to specific rules for accomplishing particular functions: armies, factories, offices, universities, clubs, and the like. Structurally speaking, organizations may be conceived as clusters of positions, each with a name and a set of rules for the behavior of incumbents. Each position, in addition to its name and the specific rules for the behavior of its incumbent within the organizational context, consists of sets or clusters of roles which the incumbent of the position fulfills in his function as incumbent. Each of these roles, in turn, may be conceived as a particular set or collection of expectations for his behavior. The whole structure is organized by rules in such a way as to fulfill a specific purpose or set of purposes.

This statement may be clarified by a familiar example. As part of the social institution of education in the United States there are organizations called universities. They consist, in their membership, of numbers of formal and informal social groups called departmental faculties, office staffs, graduate students' *Kaffeeklatschen*, and other specific names.[5] The university also consists of what is called its table of organization, the chart showing each formal position within its legal structure and the name and duties attaching to each position. One such position is that of faculty member in the Department of Sociology. This position consists of a variety of roles of which the "classroom teacher" is most familiar to the undergraduate. Now note that most of the behavior of your instructor in his class was accurately predictable even before you entered the classroom for the first time. You knew that the class would commence within a very few minutes of the hour for which it was announced in the class schedule, that the instructor would enter the room, would introduce himself, and, perhaps after making some work assignment or

[5] A formal social group is one set up according to specific rules. It usually has a name, a table of organization of some kind, material property, and may exist to accomplish some purpose or set of purposes. Informal groups often arise within more formalized ones as a consequence of needs for friendship or sociability or for the protection of the individual group members from some demands of the formal structure. Student cliques or peer groups are informal groups as are the "the privates in the rear rank" in the army. The study of informal groupings has become an important subject in Sociology. *Cf.* Fritz Roethlisberger, *Management and Morale* (Cambridge, Mass.: Harvard University Press, 1941); Robert Dubin, *Human Relations in Administration* (New York: Prentice-Hall Inc., 1951); and Burleigh Gardner and David Moore, *Human Relations in Industry* (Homewood, Ill.: Richard Irwin, Inc., 1952) and Peter M. Blau and W. Richard Scott, *Formal Organizations* (San Francisco: Chandler Publishing Company, 1961).

talking about his particular expectations for your behavior in the class, would commence to lecture to you. You knew that he would stand at the front of the room facing you and not at the back, that he would meet the class with reasonable promptness and on the days for which the class was listed. You knew that he would wear a suit, shirt, and tie, and not a kimono. You knew, if you thought about it, that he was likely to be a member of the Caucasian race who had been born in the United States of America. You knew that he would speak English, and that he would expect you to do so. You may even have known something about his lectures and his examination procedures.

The point of this illustration is that before ever seeing the particular incumbent of the particular position in question, you knew in fair detail what his behavior would be like. You knew this because you are familiar with the role of the university professor called "classroom teacher" and because that role is defined by expectations with which you are familiar even though you had not met the instructor in question. But the man who stands in front of your class every morning also plays other roles in the fulfillment of his position at the university. He may play the role of discussion leader of a graduate seminar, the role of senior adviser for a Ph.D. candidate writing his doctoral dissertation, the roles of secretary to a faculty committee, chairman of another, and junior member of another. He sometimes plays the role of counselor to students, and, at registration, the role of adviser. His position, "university professor," then, consists of a number of roles. Each role in turn may be defined by the expectations one has for the behavior of the individual with regard to that aspect of his organizational position.[6]

[6] The term "position" is here used with specific reference to highly organized social structures such as associations and bureaucracies. It is used in the same sense in which the term "status" is usually used, and "status" would be equally applicable. "Position" is used to indicate the organized nature of the roles in question. For less highly structured systems, such as social standing in a community, "status" would clearly be the more appropriate term.

The Theory of Social Disorganization[7]

Having sketched some of the basic tools for the understanding of social organization and the social psychology which underlies it, let us now turn to the theory of social disorganization around which this book is built. Rose's formulation depends upon three basic assumptions which are taken for granted and are not subjected to test.

Assumption 1. *"Human behavior is in part characterized by a social factor." People expect other people to act in familiar ways and adjust their own actions to what they perceive to be the expectations of others.*

Assumption 2. *"The social group exists . . . as a number of persons who have a set of perceived expectations in relation to one another. The expectations are either that others will behave in a certain way under certain conditions or that others expect one to act in a certain way under certain conditions."*

Assumption 3. *"The expectations (between individuals in a group) . . . specify or refer to a number of (1) meanings, and, (2) folkways or values, which together make up the culture or subculture of the group." A "meaning" is simply the definition of an object or event and usually indicates how one may act toward it or respond to it; it does not coerce one into such use. A "value" defines how one should or must act toward or respond to an object or event.*

The major features of interest in the following discussion are not these assumptions but Rose's "general propositions." The logical status of a theoretical proposition is that it is derivable through a process of deduction from the stated assumptions of a scientific theory. While it refers to the events of the objective world, it is not itself usually tested directly. Hypotheses, themselves derived deductively from propositions, are what the scientist tests directly. The general propositions

[7] The quotations in the following section are from *Theory and Method in the Social Sciences* by Arnold M. Rose, pp. 6-12, published and copyright by the University of Minnesota Press, 1954, and are used with the permission of the author and the publisher.

of the theory which define the focus of this book are as follows:

General proposition 1. ". . . *A person is able to predict the behavior of other(s) . . . most of the time, and thereby adjust his behavior to theirs . . . because he has internalized approximately the same meanings and values . . .*"

General proposition 2. "*There are circumstances under which a number of . . . individuals may be in . . . contact with one another . . . over a period of time and yet . . . not form a group, because they can make no accurate predictions with respect to one another's behavior . . .*" This situation occurs when the persons involved do not share a sufficient number of meanings and values in common and is defined as one of social disorganization.

"*We may consider two logical types of social disorganization. The first type is one in which a number of individuals . . . form discrete subgroups, each of which has a large proportion of meanings and values common to its members, but between which there are relatively few meanings and values in common.*" This form of disorganization is likely to lead to conflict.

"*The second type of social disorganization is one in which a number of individuals in physical contact with one another do not share a large number of meanings and values; that is, it is like the first type except that there are no subgroups, or each individual can be considered as his own subgroup.*" This situation is anomie and "*is productive of certain nonorganic types of mental disorder, suicide, alcoholism, and other individualistic forms of social disorganization . . .*"

"*Summary. . . . People are able to act together in an organized manner over an indefinitely long period of time because they have internalized a large number of meanings and values, commonly understood and adhered to, which permit them to make thoroughly accurate predictions about one another's behavior. Social disorganization—in the form of one or more of the familiar social problems—occurs when a significant proportion of meanings and values are no longer suf-*

ficiently internalized to guide the behavior of a significant proportion of the individuals . . . in contact."

The purpose of this book is to illustrate and elaborate this formulation of the theory of social disorganization for many of the familiar social problems fall into Rose's two basic categories of conflict and anomie.

Conflict[8]

Conflict is a social process. It was early identified in this way by the German sociologist Georg Simmel. The Americans R. E. Park and E. W. Burgess discuss it as one of four fundamental social processes in their classic *Introduction to the Science of Sociology*. For Park and Burgess, conflict, accommodation, assimilation, and competition *are* society, the things which keep it continuous and dynamic and capable of the flexibility necessary to withstand the forces of change.

THE FOUR SOCIAL PROCESSES[9]

Competition is a form of social interaction without social contact between the competing individuals. It takes the form of conflict or rivalry only when there is conscious identification of others as competitors. It is usually associated with the distributive order in a society, the division of labor, or what might be more broadly called economics. The key element in this definition of competition is that it is a form of interaction without social contact. Note the way in which the businessman uses the term, "the competition." "The competition" in his speech means those anonymous and face-

[8] This section, with the exception of quotations ascribed to other sources, follows lectures of George B. Vold, Department of Sociology, University of Minnesota, 1954-1955. Used with the permission of Professor Vold.

[9] Based on the discussion in R. E. Park and W. E. Burgess, *Introduction to the Science of Sociology* (Chicago: The University of Chicago Press). Copyright 1921 and 1924 by the University of Chicago. Used with the permission of the publisher.

less others in the world who sell the same product he does to the limited, finite public. Whosoever among these others sells a gallon of gas to a customer denies the speaker the possibility of selling that customer that gallon of gas. Any such seller, therefore, is "the competition" although not a particular competitor.

Accommodation is defined by Park and Burgess as "an alteration of function leading to a more efficient adjustment to the environment." Accommodations are always the result of conflicts, and may be thought of as processes of adjustment in social relations to prevent or to reduce further conflict. The outcome of an accommodation, then, is some kind of unstable equilibrium between the formerly conflicting groups. If this equilibrium comes to be transmitted through time it may be carried on traditionally. The caste system of India is an excellent example. The stratified structure of the Indian caste system represents an accommodation to a series of conquests carried on over centuries with each new wave of invaders successively subjecting the resident peoples of the subcontinent and pushing each group yet one step further down the social ladder. At first, of course, the subjection was military, but, as it came to be rationalized by religion, tradition, and custom, it came to represent a stable accommodation. The social order, with the exception of the economic sphere, tends to be structured by the accommodation of differences through conflicts. In personal relations these accommodations usually take the form of relationships called dominance and subordination, while with regard to group relations in the general society they take the form known as social status.

Assimilation is defined by Park and Burgess as "the interpenetration and fusion of meanings and values of one group with another and the consequent compounding of a common culture." The process of assimilation is central in the historical record of man. It is always gradual, moderate, and unconscious; it tends to be most facilitated by contact between peoples and a common language is indispensable to it. The process of assimilation is referred to in the old adage that "China has never been conquered." This means, of course, that although China has been repeatedly invaded by successive conquerors, in the end they have been absorbed into the mainstream of Chinese culture and the Chinese people. Assimilation is also the process involved in the American "melting pot." To the extent that the metaphor is apt, the United States is—or was—a melting pot in her ability to receive streams of immigrants from hundreds of divergent societies and cultures and transmute them into a society and a culture and a people of her own.

Conflict, like competition, accommodation, and assimilation, is one form of social interaction; one way in which people deal with each other. Conflict is always conscious; it is always intermittent, and it is always personal. Social contact between people is always involved. Conflict is always conscious because it is impossible for an individual to be in conflict with another without self-awareness of the event. It is intermittent because it is expensive of time and of energy and of resources. It is personal because conflicts can only occur between persons; one cannot fight ideas. Social contact, for the same reason, is always involved; one cannot fight individuals unseen, unsensed, and unknown. Conflict is always involved with social status. It has a tendency to determine the status of persons or of groups. In this context status may be defined as consisting of a position in a rank-ordering of power, where that concept (power) is conceived simply as the ability to secure the acquiescence of others in one's ideas or actions. It not uncommonly happens that competition determines one's place in a community; one's position in society, however, is determined by conflict. This does not mean that each individual must by personal conflict determine his own social location; rather the statuses of the groups and positions of which one is a member or an incumbent are determined historically by conflictual processes.

Warfare, of course, is the most severe, the most extreme, the most exhausting form of conflict in which man engages, but it also has certain aspects in common with litigation in that it is a means of deciding issues. Generally speaking, the methods by which wars are fought are determined through custom, and the issues of combat are accepted as judgments by the participants. For example, while the German people may wish they had not lost the Second World War, there is no question in their minds or in ours that in fact they did. So conflict has certain positive functions for society. It is an organizing principle of society, one way in which societies have always decided their affairs and settled their disagreements. While a certain amount of overt disharmony is clearly necessary for the existence of conflict, it gives, on the other hand, psychological relief to hostilities within the social group which might otherwise destroy it. The married pair who will not or dare not fight have only two other alternatives available to them: they can swallow their disagreements and aggressions, subjecting themselves to frustrations and perhaps to neuroses, or they can dissolve the marriage through divorce. On the other hand, the married pair who scream at each other, throw things, stomp out of the house in disgust, and occasionally even blacken each others' eyes, have available in these behaviors a means of settling their disagreements and deriving decisions about topics which must be decided—a means which threatens neither their individual stabilities nor the maintenance of the marital relationship. Bagehot's work discussed below has pointed out the function of conflict for unifying social groups; the illustration above implies that conflict has *organizing* and maintaining functions for the stability of social groups as well.

Social conflict occurs only in areas of behavior where there are no other alternatives which are equally attractive. The first clue to understanding conflict is what could be called the "principle of scarcity," for conflicts occur only about scarce values. (There are no bread riots when everyone has all the bread he wants.) Conflict is primarily physical, although obviously it has correlative attitudes. It occurs in space. (This is to say that the psychiatric use of the term, as in the phrase "mental conflict," [10] is irrelevant to our consideration here. A

[10] The reader should be aware that this is a somewhat specialized use of the term "conflict." For the purposes of this work "conflict" is used to refer to tensions between social groups where violence or the threat of violence is present, and "anomie" is used to refer to certain subjective states in individuals or to the social conditions eliciting them. "Mental conflicts" are often the concomitants of anomie. For what is probably the definitive statement of the more common sociological usage, see Robert K. Merton, *Social Theory and Social Structure* (Glencoe, Ill.: The Free Press, 1957), Chapters IV and V.

conflict to be a conflict must be objective; mental conflict is subjective and better described by other terms such as ambivalence, tension, anxiety.)

We said that conflict occurs about scarce values. There are many kinds of values which can be expanded, for example, bread, or Cadillacs, or Phi Beta Kappa keys. Social relations such as status and prestige, however, cannot be expanded and are inherently inexpandable. There is "room at the top" for only a relative few. Thus the reasons for conflict must be sought in values which are not capable of expansion. The reason for a bread riot may be lack of bread at a given time, but long-lasting frictions resulting in conflicts between groups are seldom about material items which, after all, need only be produced and distributed in greater numbers to reduce the frictions involved. The real reasons for conflict seem always to lie in interests which the participants define as irreconcilable, for whether man tends on the whole to be rational or irrational, he solves his problems in other ways than fighting about them whenever possible. While the disinterested observer might often feel the participants in a conflict have no real divergence of interest, the participants themselves will not agree (if they really thought their interests were not in dispute they would not conflict about them).

Sociology, of course, is interested in conflicts between groups. One of the earliest studies of this kind is Walter Bagehot's attempt in *Physics and Politics*[11] to explain the

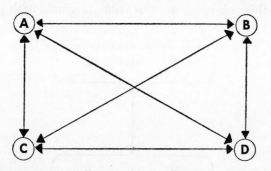

[11] Walter Bagehot, *Physics and Politics* (New York: The Colonial Press, 1900; first published 1869).

existence of altruism in a Darwinian world. The Neo-Darwinists, interested in the "struggle for existence" and the "survival of the fittest," had suggested that the typical relationship between human individuals looked like the diagram on page 25, in which the arrows indicate conflicts between individuals. Bagehot suggests that in fact the struggle for existence and the survival of the fittest is resolved in human societies through the formation of groups, with cooperation between group members developing as a survival mechanism for the human kind. Bagehot's view, in other words, is that the typical conflictual relationship between humans looks more like the representation in the diagram below. Thus Bagehot observed that the social man with the ability to get along and cooperate with his fellows tends to survive while the brute dies. The struggle for existence is not between men but between groups of men, and while the heavy-thewed, egocentric, totally irresponsible individual might seem, at first glance, to have distinct survival possibilities, a moment's thought will indicate that he would be no match for five white-collar types who had made up their minds to execute him.

In his treatise on social evolution, Bagehot made two other observations worth noting here. Bagehot points out that one of the consequences (we might today call it "social functions") of an external threat to a social group, for example another group threatening war, is to increase the bonds of cooperation and social solidarity within the threatened group. While this observation was not original with Bagehot

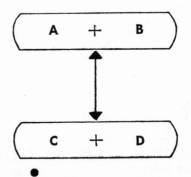

(Machiavelli had recommended the creation of an external threat as a device to permit the Prince to consolidate his power over a people, and tyrants have used the principle for ages), it may have been the first one ever stated in generalizable scientific form. It might, in fact, be labeled one of the very few "laws" of human social behavior.

The sophistication of Bagehot's observation may be comprehended by considering for a moment the practice of the modern government at war. In 1942 the United States, having troops practically nowhere in contact with an enemy throughout most of the year, solidified its widespread civilian population behind its war effort through such devices as the collection of scrap rubber, scrap aluminum, scrap iron, old newspapers, and cooking fat. Exactly what happened to all of these materials once harvested by energetic 4-F's, Boy Scouts, and housewives is unknown to the author. The rubber, which turned out to be unusable for making practically anything, was generally burned or went to waste in great heaps around the country. While scrap iron and aluminum may have been of some value to the American war effort, the dubious utility of used cooking fat collected under the "three drops make a bullet" slogan has never been clearly pointed out. To harvest usable glycerine for the manufacture of explosives from used cooking fat requires a major chemical enterprise, special plants and facilities, and highly skilled technicians, none of which were readily available for such purposes in the wartime United States of 1942. This fact, together with the somewhat stranger one that by the end of the War the United States, except only for difficulties of distribution, could have supplied all of the combatants on both sides with all the ammunition needed, might lead us to conclude that the vast civilian effort to collect fats in the earlier years was fruitless. This conclusion would be entirely in error. A nation girding up for the first time in its history for a truly total war (a struggle which was expected to last a minimum of five years) could not afford to have its civilian population supporting the war effort with any attitude other than that of dramatic urgency. The great war bond drives and salvage programs helped to provide this urgency through the demand for participation in some phase of the war effort by every citizen of any age. This patriotic fervor on the part of the "home front" population slacked off only when the external pressures of imminent invasion and slaughter were diminished by foreign victories.

The second of Bagehot's generalizations which bears repetition here is that behaviors defined as "social virtues" are apt to make for increased solidarity in the social group, while those behaviors defined as "vices" are apt to be divisive of the group. The traditional values cherished as virtues (faith, hope, charity, honesty, integrity, hard work) are all behaviors which support, unify, and maintain social groups. Those behaviors defined as vices (theft, dishonesty, promiscuity, drunkenness, gambling) tend to split, weaken, or destroy the social group.

No conflict is ever settled by conflict. A war does not settle the issues about which it is fought; the war rather settles the issue of *who will settle* the issues of the war at the diplomatic tables of peace. The immediate outcome of any conflict is an accommodation of the forces involved on the basis of some change in their relationships or balances. The political scientist's concept of the balance of power is perhaps familiar in this regard. War commences when the relations between nations have so changed over time that the balance of power (the accommodative relationships) between them no longer adequately represents the true state of social facts. When the issues involved cannot be settled by diplomacy, by subversion, or by economic imperialism, the states involved may resort to war. On the basis of the real social forces exhibited in the conflict situation a new accommodation will be struck, the combat deciding who will set the terms and what shall be the changed relationship resulting from the dispute.

One often hears when a conflict is in the offing that if we could only clarify the facts in the case, get at the real root of the troubles, some means other than force could be applied to the determination of a solution. This analysis of conflict indicates that exactly the opposite is true: that often conflicts can be prevented only by muddying the issues and that as a matter of fact the clarification of issues often makes conflict inevitable. Where the differences between the parties are truly irreconcilable, if this fact ever becomes unequivocally clear, they then have no recourse other than to violence for settling their differences. On the other hand, should the fact of the irrevocable opposition be muddied by a sufficient amount of propaganda, distraction, and irrelevance, a conflict may possibly be averted until one side or the other changes its position.

Peace *per se* is seldom the goal of the participants in conflict, nor are conflicts engaged in for the pure purpose of maintaining peace. Where peace is a goal it is always peace under the specific conditions of interest to the participating parties. Indeed some of the most vociferous pacifists in history have also been among the most militant political leaders. In fact it is difficult to describe pacifist movements without resorting to the terms of belligerency: tactics, strategy, attack, strike, move, and the like.

SOCIAL CONFLICT—A SPECIMEN CASE

Social conflict never occurs in the absence of competition. It happens only when an identifiable group of individuals moves into competition in the physical or social territory of another. Race conflict, for example, does not usually happen as a result of causes which can be removed. The races are the most easily identifiable groups in American society. There was a time, perhaps, when an Irish immigrant could be identified by his dress, speech, or manners, but that time is long since past. The American Negro, however, no matter how long his lineage on this continent, carries in his skin an identification as a member of a particular group. The different races of men seem to get along very well together when there is no competition between them. Consider the American legend of The Old South. While many aspects of The Old South legend are no more than legend, its description of the relationship between the races as amicable is not entirely false. It is true that there were a few slave insurrections in the antebellum South, but although unquestionably most of the slaves would have preferred to be free, there was little actual *conflict* between the races.

There was no "Negro Problem" in the United States until after the Civil War; there was little prejudice or conflict between the races for the simple reason that the Negro had no social existence in the white world and therefore offered the white no competition. The social structure of American society before the Civil War might have been diagrammed something like a fractured pyramid, with the Negro social world separated from the white:

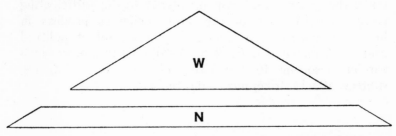

The racial problem in the United States developed when it became possible for the Negro to replace the white man. As a consequence of the Civil War, the Negro social structure was vulcanized onto the white social structure and Negroes began to compete for jobs and roles and statuses which whites could hold; then conflict between the races occurred. Conflict occurs only under conditions of scarcity. The fundamental location of racial conflict in the United States is in the American status structure. High social status is scarce. As long as, under conditions of slavery, the two races lived in different worlds, with different occupations and statuses, it was difficult for them to come into conflict; no white aspired to any social status which any Negro held and no Negro realistically aspired to any status labeled "white." Just as today (under normal conditions) it would be socially impossible for most college graduates to conflict with any other class of individuals for positions as garbage collectors, so before emancipation whites and Negroes found conflict impossible.

This dating of the racial problem does not imply that

race conflict occurred solely as a consequence of the Civil War itself or that the conflict began taking place immediately after its conclusion. Some occurred as a result of long-lasting changes in the white labor force which would probably have taken place as a consequence of industrialization even without the war (as white sharecroppers and small freeholders were driven off their lands by the demands both of the burgeoning industry and of mechanized agriculture). Others have been the consequence of the unionization of certain segments of the southern white labor force. The labor unions hesitated for many years before breaching caste lines in the South and even today are largely segregated organizations there. Unionization has often had the effect of making "white men's jobs" out of occupations which were once "nigger work" and thus driven the Negro to the bottom of the occupational ladder. This situation is perhaps best illustrated by the case of the free Negro artisans who dominated certain of the building and like trades in some areas of the South before emancipation, thus "contaminating" these occupations so that they were not practiced by whites. The long-run changes wrought by the Civil War were generally to create conflict first by the movement of whites into "Negro" occupations and then, in recent times, the reverse movement.[12]

We have indicated that scarcity is one clue to the analysis of conflict. Two other clues are the possibilities of identification and of replacement. After the Civil War the Negro became a potential replacement for the white in jobs and statuses in society. He was, furthermore, an *identifiable replacement*. If a value is not scarce, conflict over it does not occur; if the replacement of one group by another is impossible, conflict does not occur between the groups. And finally, if the identification of individuals as competitors or rivals is not possible, no conflict can occur with them. After the Civil War the Negro had to compete with the white for scarce values. It was possible for him to replace the white with regard to access to those values, and he was identified as a member of a lower status group. Conflict became inevitable.

[12] For further details see Gunnar Myrdal, *An American Dilemma* (New York: Harper and Brothers, 1944), especially Chapters 5, 8, and 9-14.

What Gunnar Myrdal calls "The White Man's Rank Order of Discriminations" illustrates the way in which conflict analysis may be applied to the American scene:[13]

Rank 1. *Highest in this order stands the bar against inter-marriage and sexual intercourse involving white women.*

Rank 2. *Next come the several etiquettes and discriminations which specifically concern behavior in the personal relations. (These are the barriers against dancing, bathing, eating, drinking together, and social intercourse generally; peculiar rules as to handshaking, hat lifting, use of titles, house entrance to be used, social forms when meeting on streets and in work, and so forth. These patterns are sometimes referred to as the denial of "social equality" in the narrow meaning of the term.)*

Rank 3. *Thereafter follow the segregations and discriminations in the use of public facilities such as schools, churches, and means of conveyance.*

Rank 4. *Next comes political disenfranchisement.*

Rank 5. *Thereafter come discriminations in law courts, by the police, and by other public servants.*

Rank 6. *Finally, come the discriminations in securing land, credit, jobs, or other means of earning a living, and discriminations in public relief and other social welfare activities.*

Calling this "a rank order" of discrimination means that the intensity of the conflicts on each level, the dearness of the values, and the degree to which they will be defended, decrease from first to last. The greatest conflicts between Negro and white in the United States occur in ranks one and two, marriage and sex relations and the etiquette of personal relations, because in these behaviors social equality is clearly implied. If an individual can freely mate and marry with members of another group, then he is indeed equal. Similarly, if people eat together as equals, then they *are* socially equal. (Eating together is almost universally considered a sign of social equality among human beings.) The emotions gen-

[13] From Gunnar Myrdal, *An American Dilemma* (New York: Harper and Brothers, 1944), pp. 60-61. Copyright 1944 by Harper and Brothers; used with the permission of the publishers.

erated by the segregations and discriminations in the latter part of the list are less intense than those produced by the former because the replacement of whites by individuals identifiable as members of the Negro group is less likely. Therefore the entire issue is less sensitive. To permit the Negro to hold a job, to own property, to receive credit, to make his livelihood, or to have equal access to the services of the courts and to the police does not necessarily imply that he can, in doing these things, replace the white. The Jim Crow system is a means of permitting them without permitting competition with the white. Only in personal relations and marriage and sexual relations, however (where competition would necessarily imply replacement), is conflict so intense that they become the areas of greatest sensitivity on both sides.

Contrary to first impressions, there is no objection in this country to a close association between white and Negro people. There has never been any particular objection (on the part of the white) to even the most intimate association with the Negro so long as he is clearly labeled as the inferior partner in the interaction. Status is the variable that structures the interaction between the white and the Negro and it is the only such variable. The subordinate status of the Negro is rationalized by saying that he is uneducated, inferior, dirty, diseased, and so on, and therefore whites cannot eat with Negroes or otherwise treat them as social equals. Yet whites commonly eat food prepared by Negro hands and served by them. It was customary among the past aristocracy of the American South to have Negro wet nurses for their babies, and it is still possible to find an intimate sexual association between the races. But in every case the Negro partner to the interaction is labeled as the inferior. Intimacy is not the major element that constitutes a threat and physical intimacy is not the threat the white sees. Neither is miscegenation, for as a matter of fact whites have always been responsible for most of the miscegenation which occurs. The issue is not racial mixing; it is the mixing of what is called "Negro blood" with "white blood" which would imply sexual relations between white women and Negro men—a clear demonstration of social equality. Thus status structures the association, not hygiene or biological differences. The rationalization about objectionable personal characteristics of Negroes is heard only when the status system ceases to operate. Negro butlers and Negro maids and Negro cooks are not dirty or smelly or diseased so long as they are servants. It is only when the possibility exists that he will cease to be a servant that the Negro becomes physically objectionable.

The notions of identification, scarcity, competition, and replacement illuminate the analysis of conflict. When whites object to sitting on the bus with the same Negroes who care for their children, cook their food, and clean their homes, it is clearly nothing about the Negro *individuals* that is feared. There is something else in operation, and when behaviors with regard to race are analyzed according to these four concepts—scarcity, identification, competition, replacement—it is plain that the "something else" is social status. Status is the scarce value and the Negro is an *identifiable* competitor for that value. For this reason conflict will occur.

The conflict has seldom been an economic matter. Historically the Negro was not an economic competitor of the white in the United States. The two came into direct economic competition only rarely. Generally speaking, the American occupational structure kept the races separated through the concept of "white mens' jobs and black mens' jobs," and since this structure kept them from competing, economic discriminations have been little practiced.

Anomie

A second form of social disorganization is *anomie*. In anomie, each individual is his own subgroup, so to speak, and the ties between the individuals are so tenuous as to be insignificant. The anomic individual is isolated and shares few meanings and values with other individuals.

The term "anomie" was used by the French sociologist Durkheim to refer to a mental state of normlessness, of being without values to structure one's behavior. (One attends college because he holds some value which makes such an expenditure of time and money worth it to him. The reasons why "it is worth the effort," of course, are various. One may be learning an occupation, hunting for a husband, doing all kinds of things, but for *some* reason college is worth it; one has the value which structures one's behavior.) The anomic person does not have such values to direct his behavior. His mental state or attitude is one of hopelessness, and he has a sense of meaninglessness and futility in life, the frame of mind suggested by Housman's famous lines about finding himself "a stranger and afraid in a world [he] never made." This is anomie.

The anomic individual is thus in a situation in which the norms that usually regulate behavior (not only the "you shalls" and the "you shall nots," but also the norms that prescribe when to wear shoes and when to wear sandals, and like choices), and thereby describe the expectations made upon one *for* his behavior, are entirely absent or have become ineffective. Under such circumstances the behavior of other people is unpredictable to the individual involved; since he is unaware of a general pattern of expectation, he cannot predict how others will behave nor direct his own behavior since he lacks expectations for it with which to guide himself. Thus the anomic individual lives in a world without direction or purpose or sense of any concern of others for his actions, and he may sink into a state of apathy and despair. A common complaint of the anomic personality is "No one cares; it doesn't matter what I do because no one cares about me."

A necessary consequence of anomie is isolation from others (whether physical or mental): estrangement from group membership with its reinforcing functions of support and solidarity, and its norm-providing behavioral expectations. Primarily, the anomic personality does not know how to behave or what to do with himself because no one cares how he behaves or expects him to behave in any particular way. He has no group to expect certain behavior from him and, therefore, does not know what to do. Secondly, the anomic personality is unable, largely for lack of social reinforcement and support, to regulate and organize his own behavior for himself. It is possible for individuals to live in isolation and still have organized lives if they have sufficiently internalized the meanings and values they once learned from others so as to go on regulating their own behavior.[14] But some persons are unable to do this, are not sufficiently strong in character to continue to regulate their own behaviors according to an internalized set of principles learned in the past. Most people need the reinforcement of social groups to keep behaving in a consistent way. An excellent if imaginary example of the individual who *can* regulate his own behavior without the immediate support of the social group is the stereotypical Englishman who dresses for dinner in the jungle. This hypothetical man does not need the suport of a group to direct his actions because he has internalized the norms of how people "ought" to behave.

Thus anomie is a situation where the social controls, the regulatory principles, normally provided by group membership are absent. When they are absent and the individual is unable to meet circumstances through his own resources of character or moral strength, he has become anomic. Anomie may also result from the adherence of the individual simultaneously to two or more contradictory, incompatible, or conflicting values about the same behavior, with the consequence that he becomes frustrated or anxious and unable to predict the behavior of others or direct his own behavior consistently. Such a conflict of *values* should not be confused with the *group* conflicts Rose describes.[15]

[14] These are the people that Riesman calls the "inner directed"; see David Riesman, *et al*, *The Lonely Crowd* (New Haven: Yale University Press, 1950).
[15] See footnote 10, page 24.

Chapter II

THE DISORGANIZED INDIVIDUAL

The reader having been introduced to the theoretical tools for analysis of social disorganization and the interaction situations which may be defined as disorganized, we may now turn to examples of the theory's application in the analysis of actual social behavior. The theory is applied to—analyzes phenomena at—several different levels of social organization: the individual, the group, the organization, and the society. This chapter considers the disorganized individual and examines several forms of personality disorganization. Remember the theoretical framework: *social disorganization* consists of a kind of situation, or a *form* of social relationship. *Social problems* are the *consequences* in human behavior of the existence of situations of this kind. This chapter discusses the social problems of anomie, suicide, drug addiction, alcoholism, and the functional mental disorders.

Anomic Isolation: The World of Furnished Rooms

A situation of anomic isolation (or an environment almost guaranteed to produce it) is what Zorbaugh calls "The World of Furnished Rooms." [1] The World of Furnished Rooms is an area of cheap rooming houses and apartments and apartment hotels on the edges of the downtown within the boundaries of "Zone II" of the American city. The sociological adjectives describing it are "blight" and "substandard." (The terms refer to an area of incongruous functions and substandard housing and other facilities.) In some

[1] Harvey W. Zorbaugh, *The Gold Coast and the Slum* (Chicago: University of Chicago Press, 1929).

great metropolitan areas, especially those old enough to have had considerable experience in rebuilding their oldest sections, this rooming-house district consists largely of dwellings constructed especially for rooming-house purposes. In most cities, however, particularly those not old enough to have torn down and rebuilt Zone II, the World of Furnished Rooms consists at least partly of buildings that were originally constructed for other purposes: private homes, often once-palatial mansions: the great ornate Victorian homes of the lumber, cattle, oil and railroad barons of the last century. New York's famous brownstones, for example, are dwellings of this kind: large deteriorated houses consisting of a number of huge rooms which have been partitioned into rabbit-warrens of one- or two-room apartments.[2] In some places the original appointments of the houses are visible; the woodwork and even the tapestries and carpets with which the buildings were originally furnished may still be present. When they are, they often show startling contrasts to the squalor of their present state: entrance halls of Italian marble, sweeping colonnades and staircases, brocade hangings, mildewed and moth-holed, or twenty-foot windows with leaded panes, and black sheet-metal mailboxes clustered like swarming bees upon the wall.

The population of this jaded area accounts in part for its architectural characteristics. On the average, its inhabitants are young (64 per cent of individuals sampled in one study were under 39);[3] they are single (only about one-third were married); they are dominantly male (63 per cent). The population is also socially isolated: of the people studied by Dr. Cohen, even though two-thirds were single, over half had no steady companion of the opposite sex and a quarter of them neither wrote nor received any personal letters in the space of a calendar year. They are indeed an isolated group.

[2] The university student will likely recognize the existence of a miniature "World of Furnished Rooms" in some quarter bordering his university and catering to the housing of students. Most American universities support such districts on a small scale.

[3] This and the following figures are from Lillian Cohen, "Los Angeles Rooming-House Kaleidoscope," *American Sociological Review*, 16:3, June 1951, pp. 316-326.

They are also an extremely mobile group. The particular sample of rooming houses that she studied had a turnover of one hundred per cent in the space of 120 days; in that short time its population was numerically replaced. Between a third and a half of the residents were unemployed. There was much mobility on the part of the rooming-house keepers as well. (Typically the people who keep rooming houses, collect the rent, sweep the hall—if it gets swept—are not the owners. The keepers are hired custodians. Cohen found that 50 per cent of rooming-house keepers studied had held their jobs less than six months.) Finally, there is little contact between the roomers and the keepers. It is not uncommon for a keeper not to know his tenants' names, or even what they look like. The greatest single characteristic of the population of the area is *anonymity*. The people of the world of furnished rooms are persons without names, without faces, and without attachments. They come and no one knows from where; they stay and no one knows that they have stayed; they go and no one knows where they have gone.

That this characteristic anonymity of the residents of the area can sometimes reach astonishing degrees is indicated by the following personal experience of the author:

During my undergraduate days I worked for a time as a private investigator in a large midwestern city. The firm by which I was employed was given the assignment of locating a wife-deserter. We were sent a recent snapshot of the man, a complete physical description of him and his automobile, and a local address about six months old. He was a door-to-door salesman of vacuum cleaners, machines of a type not found in retail outlets. The vendor buys them at wholesale from the supplier and then sells them for whatever he can get, the difference being his profit.

We traced the man to a furnished apartment in the rooming-house area of the city. He had left this address, only two weeks before, and we ran into a blank wall. We interviewed the rooming-house keeper, a relatively recent arrival in the house herself, and all twenty-three other residents of the building. In the neighborhood we spoke to gas-station attendants, waitresses and countermen at beaneries, and all storekeepers within the surrounding blocks. The investigation produced absolutely no information. Of the almost one hundred persons interviewed, shown photographs, and given descriptions of the man, not one remembered him or could identify him.

One tentative identification of his car was given by a filling-station attendant. This attendant was able to recall vaguely that a man in a car of the approximate age, color, and probable make of that owned by our quarry had several times purchased gasoline from him and that he habitually carried some kind of machinery, possibly vacuum cleaners, in the rear seat of his automobile.

In the rooming house where the man we sought had lived for five weeks, more than half of the roomers were new since his departure from the address and therefore could have had no contact with him, while none of those whose tenure in the building overlapped his could recall ever having seen or spoken to him. Even the keeper had never seen the man in question, for she knew him only as "probably the man in number 14," who had arranged to rent the room by phone and always paid his rent by slipping it under her door as he passed. He had left without notice or forwarding address and with his rent four days in arrears. The local wholesaler of the vacuum cleaners had not seen him for several weeks, and, as far as we could determine, he had simply disappeared from the face of the earth.

In fact, it is not inaccurate to say that as far as there being any objective awareness of him among the residents of the area, our man had never appeared on the face of the earth at all. In terms of the impression which he made upon his neighbors, of evidence of his existence which he left behind him, of memories of contact with him retained by others, it was as if he had never really existed.

While this case may be extreme, it is not untypical of the world of furnished rooms. The rapid mobility of the inhabitants and the total anonymity of the area permit the individual to live as he pleases and to come and go as he wishes; but they also cut him off from any significant contact with other people, and make him an isolated person, with no one to care if he lives or goes to jail or dies. The frequent conse- quence of this state of affairs is the creation of the condition of *anomie*, of lives of quiet desperation and despair, often leading to the personal disorganizations which we will con- sider next: suicide, drug addiction, and alcoholism.

Suicide, Drug Addiction, and Alcoholism

A conventional definition of suicide is "the inten- tional taking of one's life or the failure, when possible, to save oneself when death threatens." [4] In this country suicide is popularly regarded as the last desperate act of an in- dividual in the depths of anguish or despair, a terminal act to end permanently the frustration of a life no longer worth living. Indeed it is this form of it in which we are interested in this case: self murder by a disorganized personality. Never- theless, there are other forms of the act besides this anomic one, for it may be undertaken as an expression of individuality (egoistic suicide), or as an expression of strong feelings of attachment to and solidarity with a social group (altruistic suicide). These distinctions were originally drawn by Emile Durkheim, who also made note of wide cultural and other differentials in suicide rates.

Durkheim discusses the act of suicide as an expression of the relationship between the individual and the social group. In the case of the egoistic suicide, the individual has internal- ized and personalized certain values to the point where they are more important to him than any negative value placed on suicide, and his act, thus, *is* an expression of himself. An example of an egoistic suicide would be a student who kills himself because he has failed to gain entrance to medical school and prefers death to the necessary readjustment of hopes and expectations his failure entails. In the case of the altruistic suicide, the individual expresses his high degree of solidarity and identification with a group by suicidally leaving

[4] Ruth S. Cavan, *Suicide* (Chicago: University of Chicago Press, 1928), p. 3.

● 41

it. An excellent example of altruistic suicide was the Japanese *kamikaze* pilot of World War II. An anomic suicide, on the other hand, results from an estrangement from group values and support, or an inability to integrate those values without the presences and assistances of others. The individual who kills himself because his life seems utterly meaningless and to contain an excess of loneliness and despair is an anomic suicide. Durkheim describes it in this way: "[Anomic suicide] results from man's activities lacking regulation and his consequent sufferings." [5] Durkheim's general thesis is that the suicide rates in given social groups vary inversely with the degree of social and psychological integration of those groups—the strength of the ties that bind men to their societies. The weaker these social bonds within a group, the higher the suicide rate among its numbers. [6]

Gibbs and Martin have recently conducted empirical tests of this proposition (using measures of "status-integration," or role-conflict, as the operational expression of "solidarity"), and conclude that suicide rates *can* be predicted from such measures of social solidarity, thus supporting the theory with quantitative evidence. [7] The point of the Gibbs-Martin investigation is that certain occupational categories, such as bartenders, traveling salesmen, and movie stars, by the nature of the functions demanded of individuals filling such roles, disorient their incumbents to the role-behaviors other of their statuses demand of them, or estrange them from these role-behaviors. It is expected, for example, that a married man will stay home at night, cleave to his spouse, spend some time pottering around the house, and in general behave like a married man. But the bartender is out until all hours (often drinking) every night. The traveling salesman is home

---

[5] Emile Durkheim, *Suicide*, translated by John Spalding and George Simpson (Glencoe, Illinois: The Free Press, 1951), p. 258.

[6] The ubiquity of this generalization is indicated by the fact that studies of suicide tend to show that almost any factor which weakens social relations between persons, even place of residence in a city, may affect suicide rates. Cf. Calvin Schmid, "Suicides in Seattle, 1914-1925," *University of Washington Publications in the Social Sciences*, 5:1, October, 1928.

[7] Jack P. Gibbs and Walter T. Martin, "Status Integration and Suicide," *American Sociological Review*, 23:2, April 1958, pp. 140-147.

only occasionally, and the movie star may be gone on location for months at a time during which time he is expected by the nature of his occupation to make love to other people besides his spouse. In these ways stresses are introduced into the normal lives of individuals which make it more difficult for them to fill the obligations of whatever statuses they occupy. Under Durkheim's theory, people in such situations might be expected to have somewhat higher suicide rates than others, and it appears from the work of Gibbs and Martin that this expectation is realized.

DRUG ADDICTION

Like suicide, drug addiction is fundamentally social in nature, and probably, like suicide, different causes can be discovered for it. The behavior has been little studied by sociologists, however, and still awaits its Durkheim to put it into theoretical perspective.[8] We do know that the use of drugs for narcotic, religious, and medicinal purposes is thousands of years old, and is subject to considerable cultural determination. It seems probable that the American attitude to them and their use has been powerfully influenced by two events: the fairly extensive smoking of opium in the nineteenth-century criminal underworld, and the Harrison Act of 1914 which made the use of drugs without a physician's prescription illegal, and the user by definition a criminal, thus identifying him with the underworld. That this was not always the attitude is indicated by the fact that drugs were sold extensively in "drug stores" during the nineteenth century, and were present in a large variety of patent medicines. Their use in these ways was subject to little or no public censure. People took opium in somewhat the same way in which they now take aspirins, antibiotics, or tranquilizers, al-

[8] This is not to ignore Lindesmith's definitive work which attempts to explain *how people become* drug addicts. Lindesmith does not, however, attempt to explain *why* they become addicts in the sense in which Durkheim explained suicide as a function of the relationship of the individual to the group. See Alfred R. Lindesmith, *Opiate Addiction* (Bloomington, Indiana: Principia Press, Inc.) 1947.

though its use was probably not as extensive as is the use of these in the modern world.

The factors which motivate individuals to become drug addicts are not clearly understood. It may be that Durkheim's categories (egoistic, altruistic, anomic) might apply, for the process of becoming a drug addict, as distinguished from *motivation* for doing so, is known to be fundamentally social, and is in many cases, especially among juveniles, entered upon to demonstrate or to participate in group solidarity. The social nature of addiction is indicated by the reasons for it given by drug addicts themselves (see the table). While self-

Reasons Given by 1,068 Drug Addicts for Their Addiction[9]

	Per Cent
Influence of other addicts	61.5
Self medication for relief of pain	27.2
Previous use in medical treatment	3.7
Relief of emotional distress	3.1
Curiosity	2.9
Other	1.6
Total	100.0

[9] Bingham Dai, *Opium Addiction in Chicago* (Shanghai: The Commercial Press, 1937). Printed with the permission of the author.

explanation must be taken cautiously, the fact that 61 per cent of the addicts studied *reported* their addictions as due to the influence of others is in itself significant. Note, too, the very small proportion claiming that their addiction began in the course of medical treatment, a popular explanation about the way in which people become addicts. If the table is even reasonably reliable, an overwhelming proportion (nearly 95 per cent) of addicts expose themselves to addiction voluntarily and perhaps knowingly: the self-admitted reasons given by the addicts—aside from "previous use in medical treatment" and "other," a total of 5.3 per cent—all acknowledge that their addiction is essentially voluntary.

While we do not have specific knowledge of the motivating factors for entrance into addiction, we do have some excellent descriptions of the process. Howard S. Becker's "Becoming a Marihuana User" is one of these. (We must note, of course, that marijuana is *not* a narcotic drug, is *not* habit forming, and does not create withdrawal symptoms or ineradicable cravings in its user. Its use is primarily recreational, but the process by which the individual *learns to use* marijuana is very similar to that in which narcotic addicts learn their behaviors.[10])

The novice does not usually "get high" the first time he uses marijuana, perhaps because he does not know how to use it "properly." Marijuana cannot be smoked like tobacco in order to produce a narcotic effect. When it is smoked like a tobacco cigarette, no particular sensation ensues. For a marijuana cigarette to produce narcotic effect the smoke must be deeply inhaled to the farthest recesses of the lungs, along with quantities of air. This procedure is very important in the process of becoming a marijuana user, for if the product is smoked improperly and no reaction ensues, the experimenter is unlikely to continue his use of it. The first step in the sequence of becoming a marijuana user, therefore, must be learning the proper smoking techniques. The learning, obviously, can take place only in the company of other marijuana users who act as teachers.

Even after learning the techniques of smoking the drug, the new user may not be aware of its effects; he may not recognize his symptoms and reactions as those of "being high" from the marijuana. Thus in order for a person to "be high" from the smoking of marijuana three elements in the process must be present: (1) the presence of marijuana properly smoked; (2) the presence of the symptoms of the use of marijuana; and (3) recognition of the symptoms as a consequence of the possession and proper smoking of the product. It often takes a user some time to learn to recognize all of

[10] The following discussion follows Howard S. Becker, "Becoming a Marihuana User," *American Journal of Sociology*, lix:3, November 1953, copyright 1953, The University of Chicago Press. Used with the permission of the author and the publisher.

the symptoms which may accompany his use of the drug. Some of these, for example, are a feeling of cold in the extremities of the body, extreme hunger, "rubbery" limbs, mild euphoria, heightened sensitivity to external stimuli, some kind of diminution of time sense or of the awareness of time, dizziness, and tingling. Since many of these seem to be in no way related to the use of the drug or to the experience of "being high" on alcohol, the user frequently has to be taught what to look for and expect.

The final step in becoming a user of marijuana is the identification of these effects as enjoyable or pleasurable sensations, and as reactions to be sought. Marijuana-induced sensations are not automatically pleasant, as may be seen from the preceding list. They may, in fact, be unpleasant, or ambiguous, or even frightening to the new user. A taste for them, like so many tastes, must be acquired socially. Many people have not liked, upon first meeting, the tastes of onions, oysters, grapefruit, or dry martinis. In exactly the same way that one learns that onions and martinis are tasty and produce enjoyable sensations, the user of marijuana learns from other users that the effects produced by the drug are desirable. He also learns how to regulate his intake in order to avoid the gross reactions. When he has completed this learning, he may be said to be a "user" of marijuana.

The entire process is social throughout: (1) it is entered into in all probability for social reasons (few people become habitual marijuana users as a result of curiosity alone; most do so to impress friends, to indicate solidarity with a peer group, or for like reasons); (2) the techniques of marijuana smoking can be learned only from other marijuana users; (3) the user must learn, from other users, to identify the effects of the drug on his own sensations and behavior; and (4) he must learn to accept the definitions of other users of these as pleasurable and desirable.

The process of becoming a dope or narcotic addict seems to be similar to the process of becoming a marijuana user, except that in the case of the narcotic addict the pleasurable effects produced by the use of the narcotic, if any, are not his only goal. Most commonly, a person becomes addicted when the avoidance of withdrawal symptoms becomes an important stimulus for the further use of drugs. For it is possible to take narcotic drugs without experiencing addiction, so long as the withdrawal effects, which are physiological, are not identified as consequences of the failure to take further drugs. When the user identifies the withdrawal symptoms as due to a lack of drugs and takes more drugs in order to avoid them, he has become a drug addict. There are many cases on record of persons who have taken large doses of narcotic drugs without incurring addiction because they did not associate the discomfort of withdrawal symptoms with the absence of narcotics. Further, the narcotic user seldom experiences uplift or buoyancy (being "high") with drugs unless he is taught to expect it. Note, in this regard, that it is possible for individuals to become addicted to almost anything. There were newspaper reports in 1959 of an outbreak of *water* addiction in London. Addiction is apparently a psychiatric process, not a physiological one.

There is evidence to indicate that some dope addicts may be disorganized personalities, seeking escape or relief from their problems in the euphoria of narcotics. The evidence on marijuana and the reasons given by dope addicts for their addiction call this possibility into question. What *is* certain is that dope addicts are disorganized (by definition) in their persistence in socially unacceptable behaviors, and that their addiction can certainly *create* social problems, especially with regard to economic and marital matters. Since most addicts have no legal source of supply for their addiction, the only narcotics available to them are illegal ones and the cost of them is exorbitant. A five-pound sack of pure high-grade heroin, worth half a million dollars on the American underworld market, is worth only about twenty dollars in any drug store. A "thirty-pound monkey"—a big habit—may cost its owner twenty to forty dollars a day to feed. Addiction, thus, may be greatly disruptive to the lives of addicts; it does not create "criminality," however. Dope addicts seldom commit crimes of violence, although they may turn to robbery or prostitution to gain the money with which to support their habit. Contrary to the popular lore which tends to depict the "dope fiend" as a maniacal savage, heroin and morphine, being depressants, actually *repress* the aggressive tendencies of persons addicted to them.

The major point to consider is that the user, often *knowing the consequences*, and knowing his behavior condemned, *chooses* to become an outcast from the larger society in return for rewards sought by others like him. The social controls sufficient for most members of his society are not sufficient for him, and values which others obtain in other ways, or do not cherish, attract him sufficiently to stimulate his addiction. This is the theoretical problem of dope addiction. It is a problem as yet unsolved.

ALCOHOLISM

Like drug addiction, drinking and its occasional consequent alcoholism can be understood only as social phenomena. There are wide variations with regard to preferred beverages, quantities to be consumed, the circumstances surrounding the consumption, the attitudes of drinkers toward their drinks and drinking, and the attitudes of others toward the drinker. All drinking patterns are learned, and, like any other learning, require considerable reinforcement to become habitual. There are no universal patterns—even within a national culture. College students do not drink like soldiers, and Madison Avenue ad men do not drink like slum housewives, nor railroad section hands like physicians. Thus although drinking as a human social activity is millennia old, and is performed for an infinite variety of purposes—social, business, celebratory, religious and secular ritual, grief, and many others—a given person's drinking habits are learned in specific social situations.

Drinking is a pervasive feature of American society. In the United States, beer is by far the most popular alcoholic beverage, being consumed, on a per capita basis, at a ratio of about twenty gallons to two of spirits and wine. About two-thirds of the adult American population drink something at least once a year, with males drinking more commonly than females. About 75 per cent of American males take at least one drink a year, while only about 50 per cent of American women do. There are, further, distinct regional differences in drinking patterns. According to one study, roughly three-quarters of the population in New England and the Middle Atlantic states admit to drinking, whereas in the South only 45 per cent of the persons queried will say so. While accuracy of reporting undoubtedly affects these figures, they probably represent real differences. Generally speaking, younger people drink more than older people, and the behavior appears to be associated with education, for greater proportions of both sexes drink as educational levels increase. According to another study, 80 per cent of male and 61 per cent of female college students drink, although there are wide institutional variations and the actual frequencies with which college students report drinking are relatively small. Only about 21 per cent of college men and 10 per cent of college women report drinking more than once weekly.[11]

Thus drinking is a widespread, variegated, and learned phenomenon, and while *drinking* and *alcoholism* are quite different things, these facts about drinking certainly suggest that alcoholism is social and learned as well. It is possible to classify drinkers into one of several categories:[12]

Drinkers can be classified in terms of the deviation from norms of drinking behavior within a culture and dependence on alcohol in the life organization of the individual. This deviation includes the amount of alcohol consumed, the purpose and the meaning of drinking as an aspect of role playing, the degree to which such drinking handicaps the individual in his interpersonal relations, and his ability to refrain from taking a drink. There are several types of drinkers: the social or controlled drinkers, the ordinary excessive drinkers, the alcoholics, and the chronic alcoholics.

[11] Robert Straus and Seldon D. Bacon, *Drinking in College* (New Haven: Yale University Press, 1953), p. 101.

[12] Marshall B. Clinard, *Sociology of Deviant Behavior* (New York: Holt, Rinehart and Winston, Inc., 1957), pp. 298-299. Copyright © 1957 by Rinehart and Company, and printed with the permission of the author and publisher.

A *social* or *controlled* drinker drinks for reasons of sociability, conviviality, and conventionality. He may or may not like the taste and effects produced by alcohol. Above all else, he is able to desist from the use of intoxicating beverages when he chooses to do so. He drinks in a take-it-or-leave-it manner. There are two types of social drinkers, the occasional and the regular drinker. The former drinks sporadically and may have only a few drinks a year, whereas the regular social drinker may drink three or more times a week.

The *ordinary excessive* drinker not only makes more frequent use of alcohol than the regular social drinker, but in addition and occasionally under stress, may consume such quantities that intoxication results. He is given to weekend binges and is the one who, at the party, can be found sneaking drinks or just having a few more than anyone else in the place. Whatever else may be said about the excessive drinker, this type, in common with social drinkers, but with greater difficulty, may be able to curtail or completely cease drinking on his own volition. Depending upon circumstances, he may continue drinking in this manner for the rest of his life, he may later reduce the frequency and quantity of his alcohol consumption, or he may become an alcoholic.

Alcoholics are excessive drinkers who have been defined by the World Health Organization of the United Nations as those "whose dependence upon alcohol has attained such a degree that it shows a noticeable mental disturbance, or an interference with their bodily or mental health, their interpersonal relations and their smooth social and economic functioning; or who show . . . signs of such development."

Chronic alcoholics are the most seriously maladjusted of the alcoholics and are characterized by loss of control over their drinking, which thus goes beyond the relief of psychological, physical or social stresses and becomes quasi-obsessive. The chronic alcoholic characteristically has a compulsion to drink continually. Of particular importance are such other characteristics as solitary drinking, morning drinking, and physical deterioration.

THE ALCOHOLIC MARRIAGE[13]

The nature of alcoholism both as a *personal* disorganization and as an essentially *social* one is clearly demonstrated in several papers on the subject given at the 1959 meetings of the American Psychiatric Association. These papers draw the following major conclusions about the social nature of alcoholism: (1) Most wives of alcoholics were aware of their husbands' drinking problems *before* marriage, but proceeded with the marriage anyway. (We speak here of nonalcoholic women married to alcoholic men, but many women are also alcoholics and the same observations with regard to wives of alcoholic husbands may also hold true for husbands of alcoholic wives.) (2) Some women marry a series of alcoholics, divorcing each when they find themselves unable to live with their problems and then promptly remarrying another with the same problems. (3) Wives of alcoholics often actively sabotage their husbands' efforts to cease drinking. (4) When an alcoholic husband finally manages to obtain lasting sobriety, his wife often develops sudden severe mental illness, psychosomatic ailments, or (most revealingly) alcoholism.

The conclusion which may be drawn from these observations is that many wives of alcoholics are governed by unconscious needs for the dependence upon them which an alcoholic husband must show. Such women have strong emotional stakes in maintaining this dependence through maintaining the alcoholism of the husband. For this reason they may constantly undermine their husbands' efforts to stay sober, or, if the husband resists this activity, develop overt mental problems themselves. Such behavior is not consciously intended, of course, and is the consequence of unconscious motivations in the wife. Generally speaking it seems probable that in cases of this kind the wife is using her husband's need for her and his dependence upon her to

[13] Based on an article by Gerald Walker in *Cosmopolitan Magazine*, December, 1959. Used with the permission of the author and the publisher.

repress her own problems and to assuage her own insecurities and anxieties.[14]

Thelma Whalen of the Family Service Agency of Dallas, Texas, has carried this analysis further by describing four common personality types found in wives of alcoholics.[15]

Suffering Susan. *Susan's primary characteristic is a dominating need to punish herself. In marrying an alcoholic, she chooses a mate so troublesome that her need to be miserable is bound to be gratified.*

Controlling Catherine. *Catherine's marriage simply expresses her general mistrust and resentment of men. Her mate is chosen because of his inadequacy or inferiority to herself. Who could be better for this purpose than an alcoholic?*

Wavering Winifred. *Winifred is genuinely concerned about her husband's problems, but has no real comprehension of them. Her moods waver with his behavior: when he is drinking she is furious and despairing, and when he is sober she is optimistic and loving. She has tremendous insecurities herself, expressed in her vacillating moods, and selects a mate who is unlikely to leave her. She knows that she can depend upon him to remain with her because he needs her so much.*

Punitive Polly. *Polly is often older than her husband and demands neither support nor reform from him. Usually a career woman, she frequently earns more than he does or has gotten him his job through her own business connections. She has no use for the housewife role and focuses her attention and energies on competing with men and proving her superiority to them by "beating them at their own game." She chooses a mate to whom she cannot lose the contest.*

It is apparent from these observations that alcoholics' wives are not always the long-suffering martyrs that pro-

---

[14] For example see William J. Browne, M.D., "The Role of Alcoholism in Preserving the Neurotic Marriage." University of Pittsburgh School of Medicine, Staunton Clinic, Department of Psychiatry, May 6, 1959; John A. Ewing, M.D., *et al.*, "Concurrent Group Psychotherapy of Alcoholic Patients and Their Wives," *International Journal of Group Psychotherapy*, forthcoming.

[15] Thelma Whalen, "Wives of Alcoholics," *Quarterly Journal of Studies on Alcohol*, vol. 14, December 1953, pp. 632-641. Used with the permission of the author and the publisher.

hibitionist literature would lead us to believe. They are often active—although unwitting—agents in the maintenance of their husbands' alcoholism. This is not a unilateral relationship, of course, for in the same way that the wife needs the husband's dependence in order to reassure herself of her own worth, strength, and usefulness, so does her husband need *that kind of wife* in order to reassure *himself* of his security and worth, for she is dependent upon him too. Both personalities have reciprocal—if sick—needs for each other. The insecure, dependent woman needs an even more dependent man in order to reassure herself of her strength and independence. The insecure dependent man needs the apparent independence of the woman in order to reassure himself of his safety and security, and the real dependence which she has upon him to reassure him of his own (false) independence. The situation, thus, is totally social and interactive in its origin and maintenance. If alcoholism is a disease, as Alcoholics Anonymous insists upon calling it, it is a social-psychological infirmity, not an organic one. In this sense the alcoholic—and his wife—are socially disorganized; they have a peculiar little psychosocial world of their own and, while they may seek values common to others, they do it in highly individualistic and unshared ways. Their "meanings" are theirs alone.

Alcoholics may be said to be "disorganized" persons, and alcoholism is an example of social disorganization, because of the ways in which the behaviors described operate to estrange the alcoholic from group values, direction, and support. The deeper into alcoholism he advances, the more difficult it is for him to share the meanings and values of his social group, the less that group has the power to impose its culture and expectations upon him, and the more isolated he becomes. Eventually his social world is entirely circumscribed by drink and he becomes its sole inhabitant and withdraws almost entirely from all significant contact with others.

The Functional Mental Disorders

That the mentally ill are "disorganized persons" is self evident, but the ways in which they are "socially disorganized" are less than obvious. In fact, some are probably not socially disorganized—although the consequence of their existence and behavior certainly may be disorganizing to those around them. To understand the distinction, it is necessary to distinguish the *kinds* of mental disease.

The various disturbances and disorders of behavior called "mental disease," or "insanity," or "mental imbalance," are generally classifiable as either "organic" or "functional" in their causes. The organic disorders are those created by actual physical damage or defect in the brain or central nervous system. These include, for example, Huntington's chorea, brain-tumor psychoses, epidemic encephalitis, traumatic psychoses caused by brain injury, cerebral arteriosclerosis, the drug psychoses and alcoholic psychoses, the senile psychoses, epilepsy, and paresis caused by syphilis. These are called "organic" because they are created by damage to or disturbance in the physical organs of the body.

The "functional" mental disorders arise out of the individual's experience or performance in life and have no *physical* causes. They exist because they perform services for the disturbed individual. They are "functional" in an analytic sense, but their being functional does not imply conscious recognition of their utility on the part of the patient. The functional mental disorders include both the neuroses (persistent, gradual maladjustments to one's self and society, resulting in *disturbed* relationships with the world) and the psychoses (marked changes in behavior, especially in the emotional and judgmental aspects of the personality, resulting in extreme maladjustment and breaks with reality). The distinction between the neuroses and the psychoses has often been drawn humorously. One popular differentiation is that the neurotic *thinks* that other people are out to get him while the psychotic *knows* they are, or that the neurotic may build a dream castle, but the psychotic moves in and takes a five-year lease. All neuroses are functional.

Technically defined, the neuroses include neurasthenia, hypochondriasis, hysteria, psychasthenia, and the obsessive neuroses. The functional psychoses include mania-depression, involutional melancholia, schizophrenia, and paranoia. In each of these disorders the behaviors characteristic of them—and which define them *as* disorders—are *learned*. The disorders themselves, in fact, might be termed as "reactive" or "accommodative," since they are reactions or accommodations to, adjustments to, the patient's environment. They are ways of dealing with problems: learned solutions to environmental stress.

It is not necessary to discuss each of the disorders listed above, but their thoroughly social nature and their theoretical relevance to Rose's schema may be indicated by one illustration from each category.

Anxiety Neuroses—Psychasthenia[16]

[*Pearson Brack was*] *a member of the United States Army Air Force* [*in World War II*]. *At the time when his difficulties began he was serving as a B-25 Bombardier in the Tunisian theater of operations. He was referred to the Flight Surgeon because on his tenth and eleventh bombing missions he was found to have fainted when the airplane reached an altitude of 10,000 feet. That something was wrong with him became evident to other members of the airplane crew who tried in vain to communicate with him over the interphone. Brack himself was aware only of having felt cold and sleepy and then waking up to find himself leaning on the bomb sight.*

[16] From Robert W. White, *The Abnormal Personality*, Second Edition, pp. 66-70, 71-72. Copyright © 1956 The Ronald Press Co., as adapted from R. R. Grinker and J. P. Spiegel, *Men under Stress* (New York: Blakiston Division, McGraw-Hill Book Co., 1954), quoted by permission of the Ronald Press and McGraw-Hill Book Companies and R. W. White, R. R. Grinker, and J. P. Spiegel.

The two missions on which Brack fainted were his first after a period of four weeks in the hospital. During his ninth mission he had sustained an injury when the airplane narrowly escaped disaster. The mission was an important one in support of ground forces which were engaged in very hard fighting. On the way to the target considerable flak and fighter opposition were encountered, but the bombers passed through without damage. Several planes flying in formation were approaching their target when without any warning Brack's plane jolted and rolled over, then began to fall. The dive seemed to go on forever. Fortunately, the pilot gained control just in time to avoid crashing on the ground and was able to bring his ship back into formation and resume the mission. During the plane's fall Brack was thrown violently against the bomb sight, receiving such a heavy blow on the left side of his chest that he at once began to cough up blood. In spite of this he was able to release his bombs on the target and the mission was successfully completed.

On return to the home field Brack was sent to the hospital on account of his injury. At the end of four weeks his symptoms had disappeared and he was returned to full duty. It was on the next two missions that the fainting occurred.

Because of the recent history the Flight Surgeon assumed that Brack might be suffering from some residual organic defect which caused his fainting at higher altitudes. This seemed highly improbable to the medical board which reviewed the case, and the question arose whether or not the fainting might be connected with anxiety. Fainting can result from hyperventilation, that is, rapid but shallow breathing which does not supply sufficient oxygen through the blood stream to the brain. Hyperventilation, in turn, may occur in connection with suppressed anxiety, an increase in rate of respiration being one of the normal bodily accompaniments of fear. The psychiatrist accordingly undertook to discover whether Brack was suffering from anxiety when flying. In view of what had occurred on the ninth mission it seemed not unlikely that his confidence had been shattered. When interviewed, however, Brack denied that he felt anxious during flights. He laughed at the idea and said that he had never been afraid of anything. He was proud of his skill as a bombardier and impressed with the importance of his work. His attitude was carefree and jocular, confident and aggressive; he wanted to return to combat flying and asked only that he be assigned to a unit which would not fly above 9,000 feet. Even when shown that such an assignment was quite impracticable he continued to demand it with rather child-like insistence.

Although the interview failed to elicit a direct admission of anxiety certain features of Brack's behavior suggested latent uneasiness. There were two such signs: his stubborn insistence on an impractical assignment, and a somewhat theatrical, overplayed impression created by his attitude of jocular confidence. It was determined to try another means of testing him, a pentothal interview. This technique, developed during the last few years, consists of placing the patient in a quiet semi-darkened room and injecting sodium pentothal, a narcotic which produces a sleepy, dream-like but talkative state. In this state the patient can be reminded of previous incidents of his life which he then sometimes recalls with all the vividness of dreams, in fact of present realities. If emotion was involved in the incident, this emotion now breaks forth in all its original strength, the whole experience being lived over again with great dramatic intensity. With Brack, however, the pentothal produced no outburst of anxiety. He described the ninth mission in great detail, talking with various members of the crew as if he were actually there again, but he remained completely calm and unemotional. The only hint of buried fear was a sort of aside in which he urged the crew to keep on going even though he himself would surely die if they did so. From this remark one could infer a deep conviction that he would die on a mission, but after awakening from the drug Brack had not the slightest idea what he could have meant.

Still unconvinced, the psychiatrist tried a third experiment. He accompanied Brack on a practice flight to observe his reactions while in the air. On the way to the field and during the early stages of the flight the bombardier was exceedingly talkative and full of jokes, showing a forced cheerfulness that sounded very much like whistling in the dark. His confidence lasted only until the airplane reached an altitude of 10,000 feet. Then he began to tremble all over, his face appeared pale and drawn, and his breathing became faster and faster. He denied feeling fear but said that he felt sleepy and shut his eyes for long moments. He was ordered to breathe slowly and deeply, by which means fainting was prevented during the fifteen minutes that the altitude was maintained. When the plane came down to 8,000 feet he became alert again, his tremors ceased, and his cheerful confidence reappeared.

It now seemed more than ever certain that Bombardier Brack was suffering from anxiety rather than organic injury. But the patient was still completely resistant to any such interpretation. The doctor might think what he pleased; he himself knew that the after effects of his injury made him faint. Under these circumstances—strong resistance and conviction of organic illness—psychological methods of treatment are clearly out of the question. The patient is not ready or able to cooperate and there is no way to force him to do so. Defending himself against the recognition of his own anxiety, he does not feel the need for help in overcoming it. The psychiatrist accordingly recommended a trial return to duty. Brack completed another mission, performing his duties efficiently over a rough target, but he returned covered with perspiration and so completely exhausted that his Flight Surgeon referred him again to the hospital. Another doctor made the diagnosis of possible heart damage. Brack was told that he should not fly again for six months, but with proper rest his heart condition would surely clear up within that time. He was well pleased with this news. The previous forced bravado gave place to a calm cheerfulness. This time the medical board returned him to the United States for further observation and treatment.

Pearson Brack left the theater of war in good spirits, but as soon as he reached home his mood began to change. Although he enjoyed his leave with his wife and child, as time went on he felt increasingly nervous and increasingly depressed. He was troubled by nightmares of falling in an air-

plane. He was also troubled by self-reproach because he had not been able to complete his tour of duty overseas, and it was this thought that made him feel most depressed. As his symptoms seemed to be increasing he was admitted, pale, tense, and unhappy, to a convalescent hospital where he found himself confronting the same psychiatrist, transferred in the meantime to the United States. He admitted at once that the doctor had been right about his nervousness overseas although he himself had not then recognized it.

The situation was now completely changed: no longer cheerful and confident, the patient felt the need for help and begged the doctor to make him feel the way he did before he ever went overseas. But as he could not attach any content to his anxiety it was decided to try another pentothal interview. When thoroughly sleepy he was told that he was on a bombing mission, and he began to talk as follows:

"Going up to North Italy . . . have to take evasive action—flak and fighters around—plenty of evasive action—got to have it. Well, the plane suddenly shook, pulled up back of three other ships, rolled over on its back . . . falling down . . . down . . . down . . . down . . . down we fell, falling down . . . falling down, fast, faster . . . faster . . . faster . . . faster. I didn't expect it. We came out of it, but I was hurt—my chest hurt bad—my head was hurting—I was scared. Me scared! I didn't think I'd ever be scared—didn't think any man could scare me. I felt our cause was much bigger. Pilot wanted to go back, but I wouldn't let him. We had a job to do. Boys . . . our boys were having trouble on the ground—our boys, our infantry—we had to go. Every bomb had to count. If we turned back they wouldn't count. We dropped them—hit the target—smackeroo! banzai!! Chest was hurting, spitting blood—didn't like the sight of blood."

It was now abundantly clear that Brack's fainting was the outcome of a struggle with mounting anxiety generated by his panic on the ninth mission. Brack did not realize this simply as a result of one pentothal experience. It was only after several interviews, one more of which included the use of pentothal, that he finally admitted being very scared of flying. "I know it now, but I didn't know it before," he said. "I know I'm scared of falling in an airplane. I am really worried about a lot of things and I don't like to admit it." As soon as he realized the full force of his terror it was possible for him to work toward recovery. He could be shown that his fear was a very natural reaction to the danger to which he had been exposed. He could realize that he need not feel disgraced by his failure to complete a tour of duty, that what had happened was involuntary, and that he would get over his difficulties. As he gradually grasped the full import of these things his depression disappeared and his nervousness subsided. He hoped that he would be sent back to flying so that he might finally conquer his fear. . . .

Brack's case displays to advantage certain of the mechanisms that are common in neurosis, notably repression and symptom formation. It also displays the embeddedness of the neurotic reaction in the personality as a whole. To understand why he could not admit weakness we have to look into his personal history. . . .

Brack was terrified when the plane fell on his ninth mission. The whole basis of his confidence was shaken by the unexpected danger. But he could not admit this shortcoming in himself; something inside him required that he should take measures of defense against the weakness that had suddenly appeared. This something inside him we shall call his ego-ideal, the image of himself as a courageous, responsible man, whom nobody could scare. The defensive process consisted of denying that he was afraid and strengthening his outward attitude of jocular confidence which, however, showed the effects of this extra strain by its forced and theatrical character. His denial was not simply a conscious concealment from others; the anxiety was actually repressed out of his own awareness. His behavior during treatment displayed precisely the sequence of events that led Freud to his original formulation of the concept of repression: prolonged resistance against admitting the presence of an inferior motive, final emergence of that motive into consciousness, feelings of *painful humiliation at such a blow to his "ethical, aesthetic, and personal pretentions," in short, to his ego-ideal.*

Brack's system of defense worked successfully so long as the anxiety did not become too acute, but when he went into the air and when the plane rose to a higher altitude the reminders of danger became too forceful and something had to break. When the physical symptoms of anxiety—trembling, palpitation, rapid breathing—became urgent, and when panic threatened to invade consciousness, there was no solution except to faint. The symptom of fainting served a definite purpose: it allowed him to preserve his ego-ideal by not recognizing his terror. Brack emerged from his faints feeling confident, sure that some organic ailment had temporarily knocked him out. Actually he was knocking himself out by still further speeding his rate of respiration until anoxia occurred. On the practice flight the symptom of fainting was blocked by the psychiatrist's commands to breath slowly. That the symptom was produced in this way, that it served an immediate purpose, and that it afterwards served to get him out of combat, should not lead us to accuse the bombardier of voluntary deception. Like most neurotic symptoms his fainting was wrought in panic; it was a completely involuntary protective device. He did not have to faint in order to be grounded. Airmen were constantly grounded because overt anxiety rendered them unfit to perform their duties. The special achievement of this symptom was to prevent him from recognizing that he, Pearson Brack, who did not think anything could scare him, had been on the brink of panic.

We are thus dealing with a man who simply could not admit to himself that he was too scared to carry out his tour of fifty missions and that he could not meet the responsibilities imposed on him by the war.

Pearson Brack had severe disabling anxieties and the learned and interactive aspects of his neurotic behavior are plain. It is apparent in the report that from the first Brack's problems acted as a defense for him: (His insistence upon a return to combat flying coupled with his request for the impossible assignment to a unit operating under 9,000 feet has the function of making him *appear* willing to continue while actually forbidding that possibility. His conviction that he had suffered some organic damage which made him faint at high altitudes further prevented his undertaking any flying in the future and he was pleased and calm when he was told that he had been taken off flying status.) Once he had been returned to the United States, it was possible for Brack to admit the anxiety of which he was unaware while in the combat zone. The report notes in closing that Brack was "a man who simply could not admit to himself that he was too frightened to carry out his duties." He found another way out: fainting from hyperventilation, which had the function both of removing him from the fear-filled situation and preventing him from recognizing his fear itself. His behavior clearly implies that Brack had internalized certain meanings and values of extreme importance to him about "being a man," "being brave," "not showing fear," "doing a man's job," and the like. These were so important to Brack that even in situations of extreme stress where other men did admit their fear he could not. Thus by removing himself, or, more accurately, being removed, from a real social situation where some men feel and admit fear to each other and thus support each other, Brack placed himself in an unreal world without the support of others in his experience of terror. He became disorganized in self-protection. Brack had apparently learned an uncompromising set of values for "adult" behavior which were totally unrealistic in the savage world of combat. For some reason (presumably explicable by his personal history) these values were so important to him that they could not be modified. Consequently, he lived in a little world of his own, lacking common meanings and values with others.

Involutional Melancholia
—a Psychosis

Involutional melancholia is an odd psychosis, the causation of which has only recently begun to be understood.

The symptoms of the disorder are (1) periods of depression and irritability followed by periods of agitation and anxiety; (2) a terror of the future and morbid concern with the past; (3) depressive delusions of sinfulness or impending death; (4) hypochondriasis and nihilistic delusions; (5) resistance to care or treatment, refusal of food, and an apparent need for suffering or punishment; (6) severe, extreme fear of death, sometimes resulting in a refusal to sleep; (7) excessive self-concern. In terms of personality or character attributes, pre-psychotic involutional melancholics tend to be inhibited and overserious, and to have very few diversions or hobbies. Their leadership abilities are generally low. Commonly they are dissatisfied with their lives but fear to embark upon any new ventures which might change them.

The best clue to the fundamentally social nature of the psychosis is the age pattern of involutional melancholics. The average age for first admittance for treatment of patients later diagnosed as suffering from involutional melancholia is between fifty and fifty-five. For men the psychosis generally strikes between the ages of fifty and sixty-five, while for women it tends to appear between forty and fifty-five. While the personalities of men and women are often very different, and while certainly different kinds of behaviors and problems beset the person between forty and fifty-five and fifty to sixty-five, these age-sex groups share one attribute in common, one social characteristic which explains the appearance of the psychosis in each case: *loss of social function*. The ages between fifty and sixty-five are when men retire and when, for most women, the children leave home permanently. Given the nature of the melancholic, that he tends to be an inhibited and overserious person with few diversions, it is likely that for both groups the loss of social function experienced through retirement or departure of children means the loss of a major interest in life.

Involutional melancholia is not an organic psychosis. In these same periods people go through an organic "change of life." But esterogenic or androgenic injections do *not* affect the behavior of melancholics, whereas these "sex hormone" treatments can help persons suffering mental instability as the result of menopausal changes. The normal menopausal shifts of mood furthermore are neither rigid nor prolonged as is the case with the moods of the involutional melancholic, so it is assumed that the behavior is functional in origin. Thus the psychosis can be satisfactorily explained only as a psychotic reaction to sudden loss of social function on the part of persons with personality structures insufficiently stable to permit them to accept and adapt to changed situations.

Somewhat the same kind of analysis applied to Pearson Brack is applicable to the sufferer from involutional melancholia. Such patients are usually described as serious, rigid, inhibited people with few interests and with little personal initiative. The disease shows symptoms of depression, fear, a sense of failure or sin, and impending punishment or doom. These characteristics, plus knowledge of the age at which it usually begins, define the social nature of the problem. Persons with a collection of characteristics of this kind are very likely to have strict, well-internalized value systems rigidly followed, and to be largely occupied, if men, with their jobs and, if women, with their families. The men are greatly concerned with doing a good job, and are ego-involved with their occupational performances; the women are apt to be totally involved emotionally with maintaining their self-images as housekeepers and mothers.

The age-onset pattern of the psychosis gives the major clue to its explanation. Men retire or anticipate retirement between fifty and sixty-five while the families of women break up and leave home when they are between the ages of forty and fifty-five. If a person has organized his entire life around, and depends for his emotional stability upon, his occupation or his children, and possesses a rigid set of values and meanings supporting such a life, he is apt to suffer severe dislocations of personal stability when these major features of his life are "shot out from under him." If these major features of life are tied into an individual's sense of worth, being unable to fulfill them may create a sense of worthlessness or sin for him which, in turn, leads to an expectation of punishment. Through the failure to command common and realistic sets of expectations for their own behavior these individuals remove themselves from active participation in social life and become social isolates with consequent personality disorganization.

Summary

This chapter has dealt with social disorganization as it is expressed in the social problems of certain types of disorganized individuals. The disorganization, although essentially subjective, is socially engendered and has the consequence of removing the person from effective social participation. It is *personal* social disorganization. Each of the cases cited—the anomic isolate, the suicide, the alcoholic, the drug addict, and the insane individual—suffers from the effects of the social situation called anomie; none is the product of conflict.

Anomie describes a situation where the social norms for behavior usually provided by group membership are absent. The anomic individual is a social isolate, "a stranger and afraid in a world [he] never made." The social problems described in this chapter are diverse reactions to this state of affairs. In one case the individual becomes an anomic personality and drifts alone in the urban limbo of the world of furnished rooms; in another, unable to contain his loneliness and unable to live without significant human contact, he ends his life with suicide. Alcoholism, drug addiction, and insanity are less violent escapes from intolerable situations, but in every case the affected persons are incapable of responding in acceptable ways to the norms of their society. In each of these cases, too, the individuals seek the social ties they lack: the alcoholic tries, with the support of drink, to be the personality he feels he ought to be and isn't, the addict finds companionship in the closed company of other addicts, and the neurotic or psychotic adjusts to his problems with the only technique of social adjustment he ever learned.

Chapter III

THE DISORGANIZED GROUP

The social problems discussed in the preceding chapter were all consequences of the form of disorganization called anomie, which produces personal problems for individuals. Disorganization in social groups may be the consequence of either of two causes: (1) their inclusion of disorganized personalities as members, or (2) the disruption of their relations with other groups by social conflict. In the latter case, the groups themselves may be highly organized, the "disorganization" in question consisting in their conflictual relations with society.

This chapter examines cases of both types. The Beatniks of California are a collectivity or subculture including several different kinds of groups. Some are made up of serious artists pursuing an off-beat muse; some are made up of bums. All share the social characteristic of *alienation* from the majority society, with the result that many of their members are disorganized personalities. The subculture of the professional criminal and the juvenile gang, on the other hand, includes highly organized groups maintaining relations of conflict with the outside world, and they represent quite different forms of social disorganization.

The Beatnik Rebellion

The so-called "Beat Generation" has received journalistic attention since sometime before the Korean War. At first "beatness" was simply the realism and perhaps cynicism of a generation of students just too young to have served in the Second World War who went to college during the

Veteran's Boom of the late nineteen-forties. Being Beat was the generalized attitude of a group who believed themselves nominated for the role of clay pigeons in an imminent conflict in which they had no interest.

By the end of the Korean War a new and more homogeneous group had made its appearance, the "Beatniks" of California. Unlike the amorphous Beat Generation which had preceded them, *the* Beats were not only resigned and cynical but were also self-consciously and rebelliously alienated from the dominant society. A bohemian movement, the Beats began to attract widespread public attention through their exotic habits of taste and dress and through their attacks on such generally accepted values as marriage, success, education, and thrift. By 1959 college students all over the country were talking Beat argot and almost everyone who read newspapers knew of the bearded and sandaled Beats. Like most fads the Beat movement has proved to be relatively short-lived and by 1961 seems to be almost extinct, but it has some unique characteristics that make it a suitable case study. For one thing, unlike many bohemian fads, the Beats have actually had some effect on American culture, particularly in their inspiring what may become a lasting art form: the recitation of verse to jazz. Their second contribution has been in their acting as voices of nonconformity in a society apparently increasingly conforming, and as the source of a noncommunist radicalism in a situation where radicalism has almost disappeared.

The Terms of the Rebellion

One of the few extended studies yet made of the Beats and Being Beat is Lawrence Lipton's *The Holy Barbarians*. This informative and entertaining book has enjoyed considerable popularity.[1] The perspective in which Lipton wishes his readers to view the Beats is the following:[2]

[1] There may be reason to suspect that Lipton's book is an elaborate gag, that he is more interested in "bugging the squares" than in accurate report-

When the barbarians appear on the frontiers of a civilization, it is a sign of a crisis in that civilization. If the barbarians come, not with weapons of war, but with songs and ikons of peace, it is a sign that the crisis is one of a spiritual nature. In either case the crisis is never welcomed by the entrenched beneficiaries of the status-quo. In the case of the Holy Barbarians it is not an enemy invasion threatening the gates, it is "a change felt in the rhythm of events" that signals one of those "cyclic turns" which the poet Robinson Jeffers has written about.

To the ancient Greeks the barbarian was the bearded foreigner who spoke unintelligible gibberish. Our barbarians come bearded and sandaled, and they speak and write in a language that is not "the Geneva language" of conventional usage. That their advent is not just another bohemianism is evident from the fact that their ranks are not confined to the young. Moreover, the not-so-young among the Holy Barbarians are not "settling down" as the non-conformists of the past have done. Some of them are already bringing up families and they are still "Beat." This is not, as it was at the turn of the century, the expatriates in flight from New England gentility and blue nose censorship. It is not the anti-Babbitt caper of the thirties. The present generation has taken note of all of these and passed beyond them to a total rejection of the whole society, and that in present day America means the business civilization. The alienation of the hipsters from the squares is now complete.

There is probably a great deal of sense in this along with some obvious nonsense. The appearance of barbarians on the frontiers may or may not be a sign of crisis for a civilization. Many civilizations have lived for thousands of years with barbarians on their frontiers and in their midst. The fact that

---

ing, but it is ostensibly proffered as a serious description and explanation of the Beat Generation and for the purposes of this analysis is accepted at face value.

[2] The following quotation and all others from *The Holy Barbarians* reprinted by permission of Julian Messner, Inc., and Lawrence Lipton. From *The Holy Barbarians* by Lawrence Lipton. Copyright © 1959 by Lawrence Lipton.

not all Beats are young seems poor evidence for asserting a new and different nature for Beat bohemianism, and many bohemians have managed to rear families of sorts and still remain bohemian. That Beats are not in expatriate flight to other shores or in resounding radical political agitation is certainly true, but that their protest is a *total* rejection of society is certainly false. In many respects their alienation and their protest marks them as direct heirs to the "anti-Babbitt caper." But Mr. Lipton's poetic imagery should not be permitted to disguise the real significance of what he has to say: (1) The Beats are *trying* to reject the society which bred them. (2) They have, if Lipton is to be believed, done so successfully in some respects.

These things alone, although they are the characteristics of many bohemians and certainly not peculiar to the Beats, make them significant objects for study. The aspects of the Beats which have attracted the greatest public attention are the mechanics of their alienation: cool jazz, cool sex, hand-to-mouth living, the search for "meaning" in poetry, and their use of narcotics. Sociologically speaking, these are interesting but irrelevant to the major issue, the reasons for their alienation. The hypothesis that the Beats are alienated but not alien permits analysis of their characteristics. The Beats may be regarded as an alienated subculture in American society and one in some respects in conflict with it. Since to be alienated is to experience anomie, they are an example of a disorganized group.

THE CHARACTERISTICS OF ALIENATION

In a recent essay, Melvin Seeman identifies five common sociological usages for the term "alienation," four of which bear on this discussion.[3] The first of these is "alienation" in the sense of *powerlessness*. The writings of Karl Marx

[3] The ensuing discussion follows closely Melvin Seeman, "On the Meaning of Alienation," *American Sociological Review*, 24:6, December 1959, pp. 783-791, and is used with the permission of the author and the American Sociological Association.

refer to the worker in capitalist society as alienated in this sense: the worker is alienated in that both the *prerogative* of decision and the *means* for it are controlled by the ruling entrepreneurs. This view of alienation as powerlessness is extended in Weber's works and in those of many modern writers. Its meaning can be conceived as the expectancy or probability held by the individual that his own behavior cannot determine the outcomes he seeks. Note that this definition is subjective in nature; it deals with what the person perceives the facts to be, not necessarily with the actual objective conditions. When present in the individual the attitude described is likely to produce a set of agonizing frustrations and is expressive of his relationship to the social order in which he lives.

The second usage for the term "alienation" is that of *meaninglessness*. Its use in this sense refers to the individual's lack of *understanding* of the events in which he is submerged, when he is unclear as to what he ought to believe because his minimal standards for clarity in decision-making are not met. An example of a situation of this nature is post-World War I Germany, where people could not choose with confidence among the alternative explanations of the inflationary catastrophes of their times. The astronomical inflation of the mark to the point where millions were required to purchase a pound of bread destroyed savings and investment capital, made credit worthless, and contributed to the collapse of the economy and the Weimar Republic, creating the opportunity for Adolf Hitler to snatch power.

Thus one usage of "alienation" refers to the sensed or perceived inability to *control* the outcomes of one's actions, while the second refers to the perceived inability to correctly *predict* the outcomes—the feeling that one lives in an unintelligible world.

The third alternative usage of "alienation" could be called *cynicism* and refers to a situation where the norms regulating conduct have broken down or become ineffective and there is a high expectancy that socially unapproved behaviors are required to achieve given goals. This might be exemplified in American society by the saying often heard in laboring groups and among enlisted men in the military services that "it ain't what you know but who" that determines one's success.

The fourth usage of the word "alienation" refers to *isolation*. This is common in descriptions of the intellectual (the dweller in the ivory tower) and calls attention to his possible detachment from popular cultural standards. This idea of alienation contributes significantly to American anti-intellectualism: suspicion of "eggheads" as potential traitors, atheists, subversives, or the like. The popular suspicion of intellectuals as people who have chosen to be isolated from common values is in fact justified to some extent, for a frequent adaptation to the isolated role is rebellion—the attempt to bring new or modified values into being. Alienation in this usage may be defined as the assignment by the individual of low values to goals or beliefs that are typically highly valued in his society.

The foregoing are four usages of "alienation" in contemporary sociology. In these four senses the Beats are an alienated subculture, a subculture rather than a homogeneous group because they appear to be a loose collectivity composed of groups with quite different characteristics but all sharing that of alienation from the dominant society. The following examples of individuals or ideologies, each representative of specific groups of Beats, illustrate their different kinds of alienation.

POWERLESSNESS

The following quotation from *The Holy Barbarians* describing Beat views of contemporary politics makes this meaning clear:

That the typical member of the Beat Generation does not regard himself as a citizen in the usual meaning of that term is clear from all my observations and interviews. He does not value his right to vote, although he would be opposed to any move to take it away from those who do. His attitude toward the ballot is simply that it is usually meaningless; it does not present such vital issues as war and peace to the voter nor give him any voice in—or control over—such important matters as wages, prices, rents, and only the most indirect and ineffective control over taxation. His choices at the polls are limited by such tricky devices as conventions, gerrymandering, legal restrictions on party representation on the ballot, to say nothing of boss rule, backroom deals, and big campaign contributions. Elections are rigged, he will tell you, and the whole political game is a shuck.

He does not have to spend a dime for a newspaper or waste reading time in order to document his thesis that politics is a social lie. All he has to do is glance at the headlines as he passes the newsstand. Or listen to any five-minute summary of the news on the radio. Or—the plainest give-away of all—look at the face and listen to the voice of any office-seeking politician on television. As for the National Conventions on television, the spectacle is too much even for the squares to take. They tuned out by the millions on the (1956) convention broadcasts. . . .

All the vital decisions, he will tell you, are beyond the control of the electorate, so why go to the polls? The decision makers and the taste makers are non-elective and non-appointive. They elect themselves and their ballot is the dollar. Moneytheism is not only a religion but a form of Realpolitik. The moves of power politicians, once covert, are now open. Even the businessman in politics no longer feels constrained to mask his motives or his methods. More and more the show goes on the boards without props and without disguises.

The voter has no control over the uses to which atomic energy is being put by the business man and the politician. Cold Wars are launched without declaration and are well underway in the Pentagon and the State Department before he is told that they are even contemplated. The war machine is fed billions without any by-your-leave on the ballot. He is presented with a choice between a general with a folksy grin and a governor with an egghead vocabulary. Voting becomes a mass ritual but an empty one without any art of healing in it. It was once a kind of popular revel at least, a saturnalia on a low and vulgar level, with whisky for a libation and broken bottles in place of ikons. But even that is now forbidden, thanks to the prohibitionists who have made Election Day their last stand and only triumph.

The voter, the Beat Generation will tell you, does not have any control even over the air he breathes. What's good for General Motors is proving to be poisonous for the American air. And what's good for the defense industries, and is conned up to look good in the employment statistics, is proving poisonous to the atmosphere of the whole globe. "Have you had your strontium 90 today?" is a greeting you will hear any morning among the Beats.[4]

MEANINGLESSNESS

The following case history from *The Real Bohemia* (the chief work on the Beats aside from Lipton's) illustrates an individual suffering from this form of alienation.

Ed is a rebel. He is a good representative of a psychological type that includes six of the men in this study. Most people would call him "Beat." He is short, has a scraggly beard, and is usually ill-kempt. Typically he wears sweat shirt, wrinkled khakis, and sandals. . . . He is an erratic worker; great bursts of productive energy alternate with goofing off, heavy drinking, and carousing, yet he has produced many pages of poems, some of great intensity and feeling.

He was born in Mobile, Alabama, the sixth in a series of eleven children. His father, a Caucasian, ran a night club and gambling casino; his mother, a Negress, took care of her family and worked as a schoolteacher. His father was an indifferent agnostic. His mother, though, was an ardent Catholic, and Ed was raised as a member of the Catholic Church. He remembers very little of his childhood. He attended both public and parochial schools and does remember that, although a good student, he was a poor athlete. Because he was not interested in religion he did not get along in the Catholic schools. He gave up religious beliefs by age twelve.

[4] Lipton, *op. cit.*, pp. 306-307.

At this time Ed's life underwent other changes. Thirteen saw the onset of puberty—and of problems. He was arrested for violating a segregation ordinance. His parents then sent him to Chicago to live with an older brother and "keep out of trouble." However he soon found some: he was arrested for malicious mischief and also had his first sexual experience.

He remained in Chicago for two years, until the break-up of his brother's marriage. Returning home, he found life in the South "intolerable." At fifteen he left home for good and went to Mexico. He stayed there a year living with a twenty-eight-year-old prostitute who supported him. Ed was happy; they were "fond" of each other, and their sexual relations were "satisfying." But he became restless and returned to the United States to become a merchant seaman. At eighteen, he jumped ship in Nova Scotia, and lived with a thirty-five-year-old night club singer. He left her after a year because, although "sex was great, she got too motherly." At twenty-one he lived with a forty-year-old schoolteacher; sex was "satisfying," but "she treated me like a tutor with a prize plant. She had a real prize plant which I smashed to bits. Then I left her."

At twenty-two, after drinking for nine years, he had become an alcoholic. Again feeling "restless," he moved to the West Coast where he lived for two years with a young actress. This affair was violent and tempestuous; their sexual relations were irregular and unsatisfactory; "We were both neurotic and weren't ready to settle down." (It was at this time that he began to write poems.)

At twenty-six Ed returned to the East Coast and worked at various odd jobs. He moved from one woman to the next; most were his age. His sexual relations were unsatisfactory; his affairs were stormy and frustrating. He went on the road, hitchhiking for the next five years across the United States, Canada, and Mexico, supporting himself by doing odd jobs and living with women. He was arrested for vagrancy, drunkenness, hitchhiking, and resisting arrest.[5]

[5] By permission from Francis J. Rigney and L. Douglas Smith, *The Real Bohemia* (New York: Basic Books Inc., © 1961), pp. 67-69. Used with permission of the authors and the publisher.

Cynicism

Quoting a tape-recorded interview with Beat poet Kenneth Rexroth, Lipton offers the latter's description of the "social lie" of the modern state which illustrates this form of alienation.

Since all society is organized in the interests of exploiting classes, and since if men knew this they would cease to work, and society would fall apart, it has always been necessary, at least since the urban revolutions, for societies to be governed ideologically by a system of fraud.

The masters, whether they be priests or kings, or capitalists, when they want to exploit you, the first thing they have to do is demoralize you, and they demoralize you very simply by kicking you in the nuts. This is how it's done. Nobody is going to read any advertising copy if he is what the Reichians call "orgastically potent." This is a principle of the advertising copywriter, that he must stir up discontent in the family. Modern American advertising is aimed at the woman, who is, if not always the buyer at least the pesterer, and it is designed to create sexual discontent. Children are affected too—there is a deliberate appeal to them—you see, children have very primitive emotional possibilities which do not normally function except in the nightmares of Freudians. Television is designed to arouse the most perverse, sadistic, acquisitive drives. I mean, a child's television program is a real vision of hell, and it's only because we are so used to these things that we pass them over. If any of the people who have had visions of hell, like Virgil, or Dante, or Homer, were to see these things, it would scare them into fits.

But with the adult, the young married couple, which is the object of almost all advertising, the copy is pitched to stir up insatiable sexual discontent. It provides pictures of women who never existed. A guy gets into bed with his wife and she isn't like that and so he is discontented all the time and is therefore fit material for exploitation." [6]

[6] Lipton, *op. cit.*, pp. 295-296.

ISOLATION

The isolation of the Beats from popular cultural standards is probably nowhere more visible than in their views on art and in their use of marijuana and other narcotics. These are illustrated in the following quotation from *The Holy Barbarians.*

What makes ritual efficacious as a personal or group therapy is social consensus, the acceptance of certain symbols and their potency within the magic circle. All music is sacred and ritual in origin but in European music these origins have long been "refined" out of it. In jazz they are still close to the surface. That anything can be orgiastic (in the Greek sense of Orgia, secret rites practiced only by the initiated . . .) and still be sacred in the best sense of the word is a concept that the official culture cannot tolerate. . . .

In more abstract music sex can be as cool and complex as the metaphysical orgasm or the hours-long mating of the hero gods and goddesses in Wagner's operas. In jazz, where the very name of the music is still identified by millions as a synonym for the sexual act itself, the kinesthetic experience of the listener, to say nothing of the dancer, is unmistakably sexual . . .

The sexual in music becomes the therapeutic when it has the effect of liberating the listener from his inhibitions, something that squares react to in jazz with fear and fascination. . . . The sexual in music becomes sacred ritual when it raises sex to the level of the . . . holy, which in turn means wholeness, integration. It is a sacrament when it is socially responsible. . . .

For the [Beats] jazz music is both a therapeutic and a sacred ritual in addition, of course, to its many secular uses. For them it makes a swinging scene out of the sexual act, before, during, and after. . . . Knowing the language of jazz, its musical language and sharing it with others in a closed company of the initiated, is perfectly in keeping with its secret religious character. Add to this its special hipster jive and you have something very like a mystique of jazz.[7]

[7] Lipton, *op. cit.,* pp. 210-212.

[The Use of Marijuana] *The euphoria that the Beats who use marijuana are seeking is not the wholly passive, sedative, pacifying experience that the users of the commercial tranquilizers want. On the contrary, they are looking for a greater sense of aliveness, a heightened sense of awareness. Of all the euphoric, hypnotic, and hallucinogenic drugs, marijuana is the mildest and also* the most conducive to social usage. *The joint is passed around the pad and shared, not for reasons of economy, but as a social ritual. Once the group is high the magic circle is complete.*[8]

These illustrations of some of the various personalities and attitudes to be found in the heterogeneous Beat subculture indicate the ways in which the different groups of Beats may be said to be alienated from contemporary society. Some few of them are probably (as Lipton suggests throughout his book) in conscious conflict and rebellion against that society. The majority seem not to be fighting against it so much as they are estranged from it, withdrawn or outcast, feeling themselves, in one meaning or another, *aliens.*

Today, the Beats form a distinct subculture—a small radical world of their own, complete with habitat, folkways, language, ideology, and even mating habits. They are clearly alienated in several of the senses in which sociologists use that word. In Rose's terms, their alienation is a sign of disorganization within the society itself, but the individuals are not themselves necessarily disorganized.

The Beatniks made their first tentative appearance on the West Coast in 1954 and 1955, hit their peak of public popularity and interest in 1958 and 1959, and now show distinct signs of decline. The enclave of Beats in North Beach has diminished as a result of the attitude of the San Francisco police, who never appreciated the "local color" they provided, and the pads of Venice West, once crowded, are reputed to be in decreasing demand. Thus it appears that the "Beat Generation" was less a generation than a fad. In this it appears to follow closely what LaPiere calls "fugitive patterns in congenial behavior," which, because they are only substitutes for true congeniality, are transitory and fleeting in character

[8] Lipton, *op. cit.*, p. 171.

and have little social significance for the individual.[9] If there is an analogy between the congenial behavior of individuals and whole societies, and if LaPiere is correct, the Beats are transitory variations on standard social themes, unique configurations of the typical American bohemianism.

The Criminal Subculture

Rose defines two generic models of social relations which can be called disorganized. In cases of disorganized individuals, each person forms an isolated social unit of his own with meanings and values so unique or so tenuous as to prohibit group memberships of significance for him. In the second model people share a sufficient number of meanings and values to permit them to become members of groups, but these groups, although in contact with other groups, have so little in common that the relations between them become situations of conflict. The relationship between the American underworld of professional criminals and the society in which it exists illustrates the latter model. This is a case of a subgroup within a society, of a subculture within a culture, with a well-established and articulated set of meanings and values in opposition to those of the society and culture which include it.

Like the folkways and mores of any culture, those of the criminal subculture are *learned* by its members, both in childhood and after recruitment into its occupational categories. People learn to be prostitutes, bank robbers, and racketeers in the same way that other people learn to be housewives, nurses, turret-lathe operators, and school teachers. The ways in which people become criminals, or members of a delinquent subculture, have been detailed by Sutherland and Cressey.[10]

[9] See Richard LaPiere, *Collective Behavior* (New York: McGraw-Hill Book Company, Inc., 1938), pp. 176-177.

[10] The following section is based on and follows closely Edwin H. Sutherland and Donald R. Cressey, "A Sociological Theory of Criminal Behavior,"

"Criminal behavior is learned. It is not inherited like eye color nor can most of it be invented by persons without any previous training in criminality. The specific direction of motives and drives is learned from definitions of the legal codes as favorable or unfavorable." In some societies the individual is surrounded with favorable definitions of the legal codes; in some he is surrounded with unfavorable definitions of them. In the United States definitions tend to be mixed and there are distinct culture-conflicts about legal codes. Such conflict is demonstrated by ambivalent and ambiguous feelings about the laws and obeying them. How many readers habitually obey speed regulations? While alternately obeying and disobeying traffic regulations is perhaps the most typical form of American ambivalence with regard to the law, the ambivalence may be more clear-cut with respect to tax evasion or theft from employers. The annual bill paid by American industry for petty theft of time, tools, and materials has been estimated at well over $5,000,000. Every secretary who takes home a pencil, every machinist who takes home a micrometer, every automobile assembler who takes home a wrench or a handful of screws has engaged in larceny. Yet, in many occupations such theft—petty on an individual scale, but overwhelming in the aggregate—is expected behavior. Even definitions of what constitutes criminal behaviors are equally ambiguous. Who is a criminal? Anyone who has ever been questioned about a crime? Arrested for a crime? Jailed for a crime? Tried for a crime? Convicted of a crime, or sentenced? Legalistically speaking, an individual becomes a "criminal" only when he has been arrested, tried, and convicted of crime. In the everyday meaning of that term, the distinctions are much less finely drawn.

"A person becomes delinquent because of an excess of definitions favorable to violation of law over definitions unfavorable to violation of law." That is, people learn the culture around them. When the child, riding with his father in the car, sees the father triumphantly run a stop sign, force

Principles of Criminology, 5th ed. (New York: J. B. Lippincott Co., 1955), pp. 74-80. Copyright © 1955 by J. B. Lippincott Co. Used with the permission of the publisher, Donald R. Cressey, and Mrs. E. H. Sutherland.

another driver off the road, or exceed the speed limit and chortle about it, he learns that it is all right or even "smart" to disregard the traffic laws. When an individual grows up in a social group that sees the police as enemies and defines all "honest" men as suckers, *these* are the definitions he learns. When an individual lives in a society which permits or even encourages petty chicanery and grifting, little larcenies and frauds in normal business and social intercourse in the name of being smart, getting away with it, making a quick buck, getting payola, and the like, *these* are the definitions he learns.

"The process of learning criminal behavior by association with criminals . . . involves all the mechanisms that are involved with any other learning. While criminal behavior is an expression of general needs and values, it is not explained by those general needs and values, since non-criminal behavior is an expression of the same needs and values." The *goals* of the criminal are usually the respectable goals of the culture in which he lives. The means that he learns to attain these ends, however, deviate from those learned, at least as major devices, by most of the persons in his society. Thus if affluence, power, and status are general cultural goals, they may be attained through racketeering or through selling life insurance. It is probably not true that most criminals have learned to value the ends they seek above the means they have learned to seek them. It seems more likely, rather, that they have learned to value certain means and to devalue others even as the reader and every individual around him.[11]

THE CULTURE OF THE PROFESSIONAL THIEF[12]

The mob has many codes, rules, and understandings, most of which are so general that they apply to the

---

[11] For a cogent and closely reasoned theory to explain why *certain* persons learn the *particular* delinquent values they do, see Albert K Cohen, *Delinquent Boys* (Glencoe, Ill.: The Free Press, 1955).

[12] Reprinted from *The Professional Thief*, E. H. Sutherland (ed.), pp. 35-38, by permission of The University of Chicago Press. Copyright 1937 by The University of Chicago Press.

whole profession as well as to a particular mob. One of these codes is that the division of all gains in all rackets is to be even. No one gets more or less than anyone else in the mob. This rule applies only to members of the mob and does not apply to outsiders who may assist the mob in various ways. The owner of a pay-off joint may get 10 per cent of the job, the put up man gets 10 per cent and the pawnbroker who works in collusion with the mobs on short con rackets may get a percentage. A second rule is that the nut [expenses] must come off the top of every touch. This means that all expenses must be deducted from the gross return before there is division among the members. A third rule is that all loans must be repaid out of the first knock-up money and this is rigidly adhered to.

A fourth understanding is more general, and it involves many different situations. It is sometimes stated "in on the good, in on the bad," and sometimes "in with the touches, in with the falls." If one member of a mob gets a pinch, and the case costs $500, each member of the mob contributes his share of it. If a four-handed mob packs in for the day, three going in one direction and the fourth in the other direction, and if the three members get a score, the fourth man is in on it for his full end. However, if on the way home a member is pinched for something foreign to the mob's activities, he stands the fall personally. Of course, if he didn't have sufficient money to take care of the case, the others would lend him any money he needed, but it would not be considered unethical for the others to move on and leave him in the can. If one of the members stands a pinch for the activities concerned with the mob, and the outfit can grift for a few days without him, he would, when he got out, receive his full end of every dollar that was made while he was in the can. It was the mob's fault that they didn't get him out. But if he should get a bit, and it became necessary to fill a man in his place, the new man would naturally get his end and the one doing the bit would not have a claim, but the mob would as a rule see that he was taken care of and that a piece of money was waiting for him when he came out.

A fifth rule is that the fall-dough held by the mob is to

be used for any member of the mob and that it is the possession of the mob. There are few known cases of a boss absconding with this money or gambling with it or losing it otherwise. He would not dare to do this.

A sixth understanding is that the members of the mob are to deal honestly with one another. One of the most heinous crimes in the mob is for a member to burn the others, that is, report that a score showed less than it actually did and hold out the difference. When this occurs, the first offense is the last. Lying is perhaps considered by thieves to be more unethical than it is by the law-abiding.

A seventh understanding is that, if a member voluntarily separates from a mob, he may properly ask to be taken back, but it would not be proper for the leader of the mob to ask him to come back. Similarly if the boss fires a member, the boss may later invite the member to return, but it would not be proper for the member who had been fired to ask to be reinstated.

An eighth understanding is that the member of the mob should not be held responsible for events which he cannot control. Situations arise sometimes where all the larceny sense in the world cannot be of aid. It is what the thieves call "the luck of the law." But if a member shows up late for meets on several occasions, that is regarded as his own fault and he may be discharged for it.

A ninth rule is that one member of a mob should not cut in on another. Each member is given his part to do and is expected to handle his own part, unless it be a case of an inexperienced man who has been taken on for a minor part. If another member should cut in, it would be a reflection on the ability of the first to handle the situation himself and would be resented as such, unless an unusual or dangerous situation arose.

Finally, it is recognized as a responsibility of every member of the mob to do everything possible to fix a case for any member of the mob if the pinch occurred in connection with mob activities.

A mob must be a unit and work as a unit. These rules

and understandings have developed primarily for the purpose of preserving the unity of a mob.

The thoroughly learned and cultural nature of *professional* criminality is apparent in Sutherland's account. The professional criminal can hardly be called a disorganized individual, a mental defective, or any like term, nor even, usually, an asocial personality. An important distinction has to be made here between the true professional and the amateur criminal. The vast bulk of criminal activity in the United States is the work of amateurs, some of whom may well be disorganized or pathological personalities, unsocialized and unsocializable, but the professional thief must be thoroughly socialized to the criminal culture and to other criminals for him to be able to practice at all. Of the estimated $30 billion annually lost to crime in the United States, a large proportion goes into the pockets of so-called "white-collar criminals" who are not professionals, but persons usually defined as law-abiding who steal money, time, or materials from their employers or the public in the course of their occupations. Embezzlement is the obvious illustration, but the petty theft of tools, merchandise, cash, materials, and time run into far larger figures than the sums annually taken by embezzlers. The amounts taken from the public every year by dishonest firms and by "sharp" practices are astronomical.

The professional thief learns a special subculture which defines his behavior and rewards it, and, since it *is* culturally rewarding, measures himself against those special standards. The white-collar criminal, on the other hand, exists in the predominantly noncriminal culture, and it is to contradictory expectations in *it* that we must look for the explanation of his behavior. In this respect the embezzler and the businessman who "sails close to the wind" are brothers under the skin. (See Chapter V.) The disc jockey who takes payola is a white-collar criminal and is closely akin to the quiz-show contestants who took their winnings under the pretense of competition. While the latter did not employ their fraud "in the course of their occupations" and are not, therefore, white-collar criminals strictly defined, the meaning of the term clearly applies to them. Since such persons do not belong to the special culture of the criminal underworld the values to which their behaviors are addressed are to be found within the general culture in its lawless aspects. Rugged individualism, the belief in self-reliance, and the use of material goods as the measure of men—all common aspects of contemporary American society—may explain such white-collar criminality.

The Juvenile Gang

THE JOLLY ROGERS, A JUVENILE GANG[13]

"The Jolly Rogers" are a high-school fraternity in a northern industrial city. They are also a juvenile gang in that their leading members engage together in activities, some of them delinquent, which are in no way related to their fraternal obligations or customs. For the purposes of this study the term "fraternity," or its name, is used to refer to the parent organization and its activities. The term "gang" is used to refer to the clique within the fraternity which comprises its only truly "primary" group. The fraternity numbers fourteen members ranging in age from 14 to 18. The gang numbers seven members ranging in age from 15 to 18 who associate almost exclusively with each other and who sometimes engage together in delinquent behavior. Its nucleus is the five senior members first described below.

THE GANG MEMBERS

Keith Johnson: *A tall, thin, 18-year-old, his face wears a sad expression broken frequently by broad, sly smiles. He slouches when he walks and speaks drawlingly but with an excellent command of language. Called "Curley" by the group (because of increasing baldness), he is its unofficial leader principally through the power of his buoyant per-*

[13] By "An Alumnus," observations *circa* 1945-1950.

sonality. Though his friends know him as a braggart, liar and physical coward, his great gift of gab, sparkling wit, and prowess as a raconteur make him socially invaluable to the gang.

Johnson is regularly employed after school and Saturday and usually has more spending money than other gang members. He claims to be indifferent to money but, while he often wins the group poker or crap games (because of his larger resources), he is reported to be a poor loser. He belongs to no other groups in the school or the community and goes nowhere except in the company of his cohorts.

He is a fairly heavy smoker and a moderate drinker. His friends report that while he claims great drinking prowess, he is apt to be the only one of the older boys left sober after an evening of carousing. He dates irregularly with a girl whom his companions repute to be a "hot rock," but the rest of the gang insist upon his sexual innocence because "he is too dumb to get to first base."

Mark Fitzpatrick: *A small wiry boy of Irish descent, aged 17, he has fine bones and delicate features which give him a feminine appearance. Perhaps because of his looks he has developed an aggressive attitude illustrated by his favorite expression: "I'll try anything once." He is the most combative of the gang and is responsible for much of the fighting and rowdyism in which they engage. It is his habit to get drunk every Saturday night and then go in search of girls or a fight on the downtown streets, activities in which he is sometimes accompanied by MacKenzie. Fitz is employed only during school vacations, and then irregularly. He works until he has accumulated twenty or thirty dollars and then quits until he needs further funds. He supplements his income by gambling and playing pool and his attitude toward money is: "Easy come, easy go; you can't take it with you." When a sudden need for cash has caught him short he has been known to steal accessories from parked cars for sale at secondhand-parts houses. He belongs to no other group in the community but is a member of the school boxing team.*

He does not smoke but is the heaviest drinker of the gang and is reported to hold his liquor well. His "dating" has

● 85

purely sexual ends and he associates exclusively with girls of the lowest social classes, with whom he makes no attempt to disguise his purpose.

Tom MacKenzie: A 17-year-old blonde of stocky build, he has a happy-go-lucky nature and is the poet-laureate of the group, having committed to memory dozens of verses and songs (many of them ribald) and composed others of his own. His happy extroversion complements Fitzpatrick's brooding cynicism and they are the closest friends of the gang. Lacking Fitzpatrick's aggressiveness, he is nevertheless frequently embroiled in battles by him.

MacKenzie earns his spending money by weekend work at a filling station and supplements this income doing odd jobs such as snow shoveling and lawn mowing for neighbors. He emulates Fitzpatrick's free-wheeling disregard for finances, but his frequent losses at poker and craps depress him. His unique position in the fraternity as the only owner of a car, a battered jalopy of ancient vintage, makes him its official bus company, a position he enjoys. The gang contributes to the upkeep of the car by siphoning gas and occasionally stealing a tire for it. Tom is a member of the school football team but belongs to no other school or community groups.

MacKenzie smokes moderately and drinks only in the company of other members of the gang. He has few dates with girls and prefers to attend fraternity and school functions in the company of Fitzpatrick and Johnson.

Bill Hodges: A small boy with unhandsome good looks, he is President of the fraternity and its severest critic and booster. He concentrates his considerable abilities on school and fraternity activities and at seventeen is President of both senior class and student council. The rest of the gang sometimes take him to task for being "stuffy," but they recognize that it is really he who keeps them functioning as an organization.

Bill is a popular member of the city's junior social set, plans to attend an Ivy League college, and dates a girl from the city's swank private academy. He does not work and has a number of home duties and responsibilities which he is careful to fulfill. He is given spending money by his parents *and budgets it with care. He belongs to a number of school organizations, attends the Unitarian Church irregularly, and has a junior membership in the city's athletic club.*

He smokes irregularly and limits his drinking to one beer with the gang except at their specialized drinking parties. He refuses to speak about his sexual experience or his steady girl, and it is the consensus of the gang that, "Willy wouldn't touch it if he could."

Paul Lawrence: In looks so similar to Johnson that strangers often confuse them, he is in background very like Hodges. An individualist in a peer-oriented group, he often finds himself a minority of one on many matters and is the willing butt of their gibes and practical jokes. He is 18. Paul, like Hodges, is a member of the city's junior social set, although he finds little satisfaction in that fact. He probably feels more parental control than any of the other older members of the gang and is often forbidden to attend their informal activities. Most of their gambling is done in his home, this being a sport to which his parents do not object. Since his parents are often absent at social affairs, Bill makes up to the gang for having to "baby-sit" with his brother and sister by having the boys in for beer from his father's stock on such occasions. He attends church with his parents but belongs to no other school or community organizations.

Lawrence smokes lightly and drinks seldom but overindulges when he does. He never goes out with girls and is believed to be afraid of them although he has been known, when drunk, to make advances to waitresses or other girls of a presumably lower class.

Kurt Siller: 15-year-old Siller is a complete extravert and is always on the lookout for a good time. He is a hard, if unwilling, worker and boisterously follows the lead of any of the older boys. His bubbling humor keeps fraternity meetings in an uproar. His particular heroes are Johnson and MacKenzie, whom he likes to accompany, but he will go with any senior gang member. He belongs to no other school or community groups.

Siller has little responsibility in the home and shirks what he has. He does not work and is given an allowance of *seventy-five cents a week. Since the fraternity meets Monday night and Kurt cannot resist the crap games which inevitably close the meetings, he is often penniless for the remainder of the week.*

He is only beginning to smoke under the tutelage of the older boys, and is not permitted to drink at any regular function. Sometimes he is allowed one beer when out for an informal night with the gang. "After all," Johnson explains, "we do not want to be contributing to the delinquency of a minor." Kurt is popular with the girls of his own school class (he is a sophomore), and dates a number of them regularly. The gang is of the unanimous opinion that he is innocent of the mysteries of sex, and Fitzpatrick has christened his naive exploits "bunny-hugging."

Herb Nadeau: A small, brown replica of Siller, many of the observations made of the latter hold true for this 15-year-old. He is in other ways more like Hodges, for he takes his fraternity duties seriously, is active in school affairs, and finds some of the gang's activities reprehensible. Herb has certain home duties which his parents expect him to fulfill but which he will leave in favor of an outing with the gang when he can. Like Siller, he is an extravert but unlike him, he enjoys carrying out his ideas as much as he does plotting them. He neither smokes nor drinks and has few dates. He is employed as a "carry-out" boy in a grocery store.

Gang and Fraternity Organization

The Jolly Rogers are a fraternity; the organization contains a juvenile gang, but it was originally founded as a fraternity, the gang recruits its members from it, and the gang members consider themselves members of the fraternity. The gang is not a crime-spawned group; it is doubtful, in fact, that the boys think of themselves as belonging to a "gang." Their fraternity has been in existence for over forty years and has developed a set of traditions, histories, and activities remarkable for a group of teen-age boys.

The fraternity holds weekly meetings conducted loosely

in accord with Robert's Rules of Order. Formal leadership is decided by ballot in which the President, Secretary, and Treasurer are elected. Elections are hotly contested with a great deal of covert "politicking" preceding them. The President presides over formal meetings and has the authority to expel members and to suspend them from future meetings if their conduct proves prejudicial to good order.

The President obtains his authority through the peer group and maintains it in the same way. Candidates for the fraternity are indoctrinated in peer-group ethics and learn that the group opinion may not be lightly disregarded. Thus, while the decisions of the President are always open to argument while they are being made, once made they are neither argued nor disobeyed. The power of the President lies in the consensus which supports his office and the group, having been forged in pledgeship, will support this power even if its members do not concur in the decisions. Immediately upon termination of the formal meeting, leadership may pass to an individual without office but with greater popularity than the President, but during the course of the meeting the President is leader, judge, and jury.

The Jolly Rogers' pledge system is the fundamental strength of the organization and accounts in large part for its long history and success. Pledge classes are opened with each semester of the school year and candidates are brought to two or three weekly sessions for appraisal. At the end of the inspection period, if the candidate is interested in joining the fraternity and the actives are unanimous in their approval of him, he is given his "pledge-letter" and pin. The pledge-letter is a traditional set of instructions in the duties of pledgeship and the pledge memorizes it. At the close of this meeting the new pledge is also given his "craphead number," by which he is known for the duration of his pledgeship. He is expected henceforth to identify himself with the phrase, "Craphead number XVI, Sir."

Formal pledge-hazing at meetings takes place after a refreshment break. The pledge reports to the President using his craphead number and stands at attention. The President examines him on the contents of his pledge-letter and the pledge reports to each active in turn. The actives question him about his assigned duties and may, if displeased with the way in which any were carried out, paddle the pledge with a twenty-inch fraternity paddle. At one time hobnailed or drilled paddles were in use, but such "armored" types have since been outlawed. There is intense competition to see who can paddle hardest, break a paddle, or perfect a unique paddling technique. The circuit of the actives completed, the pledge is dismissed with instructions to send another pledge into the room.

The period of pledgeship lasts from eight to twelve weeks, its duration depending upon the behavior of the pledge class. The final week of pledging is "hell week," when hazing reaches a peak. The pledge is given a set of difficult or impossible tasks upon the results of which he is examined on the last night of pledgeship, "hell night." No pledge has ever been successful in the completion of his hell-week duties. With the end of pledgeship the candidate is inducted into the fraternity in a candlelight ceremony and becomes an active with full privileges. If he is an underclassman he is expected to show some deference to the senior actives, but no other distinctions are drawn. The Jolly Rogers feel that when a boy successfully completes his pledgeship and is accepted into the group, he is a willing and responsible fraternity member. The function of the pledge period is to create a common body of sentiment toward the fraternity, a sense of unity and esprit, and a strong peer orientation.

After the "pledge session" the final ritual activity of the meeting takes place among the actives. This is the "bitch session." At this time any member who has a grievance against another or a complaint about the conduct of the meeting or a pledge is given the opportunity to be heard. It is considered mandatory that grievances between members be aired in this manner, and a fraternity member who has such a grievance and does not open it at this time is judged to have forfeited his right to bring the subject up again. This airing of disputes stimulates thought and pacifies quarrels that might otherwise provoke schisms dangerous to the group. In cases of quarrels between individuals it is customary for each to present his side of the issue to the group and a decision to be rendered by the President or, when appropriate, by collective opinion.

FRATERNITY AND GANG ACTIVITIES

In addition to its weekly meetings the fraternity engages in only three formal activities during the school year. These are an annual banquet for members and alumni, sponsorship of dances, and a semiannual houseparty.

The annual Jolly Rogers Banquet is the most significant event of the fraternity's year and is one of the most important reasons for its long survival. Banquets are usually held in mid-November, but preparations commence with school in September. The toastmaster is elected at one of the first meetings in the fall and upon him falls the responsibility for the banquet although he usually selects a committee of actives and pledges to assist him. The Toastmaster makes arrangements for a hall, selects a menu, makes alumni reservations, and arranges for such professional entertainment as may be desired. From fifty to seventy-five persons ranging in age from 14 to 60 attend the banquets, some of them coming considerable distances.

The significance of the banquet in the life of the fraternity lies in the activities necessary for its accomplishment. Since it is an annual affair and the fraternity toastmaster may serve only once, each year at least one and often several boys correspond with each alumnus asking his presence, cajoling it when an affirmative response is not immediately forthcoming, seeking anecdotal materials for use in speeches, and so on. The presence at the affair of men who were members of the Jolly Rogers decades before the present members were born further establishes the vitality, traditions, and organic character of the organization. The interaction between old and young members supports a sense of solidarity, unity, and purpose lacking in any of the school's younger and less well organized fraternities. The Jolly Rogers' systems of pledgeship and banqueting are its unique source of strength and vitality.

The second major activity in which the fraternity engages during the school year is sponsorship of dances. The public high school from which the Jolly Rogers have historically drawn most of their members seems to be remiss in this regard, for there is only one official "school" dance in the year. The school's fraternities and sororities have stepped into the breach and each organization has the responsibility of sponsoring at least one dance each school year. Since the organizations are illegal, the school does not recognize these affairs and does not sanction them on school property, so they are held in public halls and are open to the public. The Jolly Rogers' system is probably typical: a hall and orchestra are engaged (usually with only token payment, for the group depends upon the dance to provide funds for its own support), and advertisements are printed and distributed. The fraternity members administer the operation, selling tickets, checking coats, securing and selling soft drinks and beer, ejecting unruly patrons. Since the dances are open to the public they are usually profitable. However, because the income from such undertakings depends upon the number of tickets sold, the quality of the hall, occasion, orchestra, and the amount of advertisement, they have sometimes lost money. In one case a net profit of $300 was made while in another the fraternity had a net loss of $60.

The semiannual houseparty is the third major activity of the school year. One is held during the Thanksgiving vacation and the other celebrates the close of school. Fall houseparties are part of pledge-hazing and are usually held in a lake or river cabin belonging to members' parents or friends. They last two to four days, with only actives and pledges present. Little is accomplished or attempted, days being devoted to sleep, poker, ice-fishing, hunting, pledge-hazing, and "fooling around." Nights find half the group playing poker or craps with beer to "keep the game going" while nonplayers drink and try to pick up girls in nearby towns.

Spring houseparties are quite different. The fraternities

and sororities of the school collectively engage an entire lake or river resort for their use the week following the close of school. At this time the girls' groups have chaperones, while the boys govern themselves as best they can. The presence of girls, plus the fact that a number of organizations participate in these affairs, is the occasion for considerable drunkenness and rowdyism. Activities again include gambling, drinking, and fishing, this time with the attractions supplied by swimming, wiener roasts, and the opposite sex.

For the spring houseparty it is the custom of the fraternity to pay its house rent from the year's dues plus profits left from dances, while all members contribute equally to purchase food and those who desire drinks supply their own. Because there are no pledges at this season of the year, cooking, cleaning, and grocery-buying are done by the actives in rotation.

Houseparties are the social highlights of the fraternity's year, being regarded as pure "fun," while banquets and dances have aspects of both work and obligation. In addition to their recreational aspects, they contribute also to group tradition, for the events at them become magnified into epics of valor, comedy, and individuality. Heroes and villains are made at houseparties and pledges are firmly fixed into the life of the group or leave it in disgrace. (The fraternity became completely committed to Fitzpatrick and MacKenzie when, during their pledgeship at a fall houseparty, they consumed a quart of Scotch carefully hidden by an unpopular senior active. This exploit, being so atypical of pledge behavior, has become a fraternity legend.) Since each houseparty and its exploits are related to and compared with parties before it, each provides motivation for parties to come and becomes a part of the warp and woof of fraternity history and tradition, gives continuity to the year's activities, and ties one year's membership to the next.

In addition to these formal activities certain informal collective behaviors characterize the fraternity, largely because of the presence of the gang. One of these is gambling. Some kind of poker or crap party takes place almost weekly. Attendance is usually limited to senior fraternity members, with others occasionally invited. When possible, gambling parties take place in one of the boys' homes, when parents are absent.

In some respects these gambling sessions perform the social functions for the gang which formal meetings do for the fraternity. There are ritual elements, ritual words, expressions, and phrases, and ritualized behaviors expected of certain players in specific situations. They are in part the reasons for the gang's original formation (the specific gang members first drifted together as a gambling club), and they provide its major continuing activity.

Another informal activity commonly practiced by the fraternities of the school is known locally as the "pow-wow," or wiener roast. These are activities of autumn and late spring, and in midwinter they are replaced by sleigh rides. Again the presence of the gang within the fraternity has resulted in some unique modifications which seem to be peculiar to the Jolly Rogers: within the high-school social system "pow-wow" means a wiener roast organized by members of one sex to which members of the other are invited as dates. On the initiative of Johnson, Hodges, and Fitzpatrick, however, the Jolly Rogers have developed the "stag" pow-wow which permits the elder fraternity members to drink themselves into a stupor. Although the influence of the gang is evident in the stag pow-wow, it is defined as a fraternity activity, and the gang alone has never attempted one. Junior members and pledges are brought along to tend the fire, cook, and drive the senior members home. The preferred drink is the "boiler-maker," concocted by dropping a shot glass full of whiskey into a mug of beer. The actual dropping of the filled shot glass into the mug is always the occasion for great hilarity, the person who is going to have the drink being required to do his own mixing as a "sobriety test." When he can no longer hit his mug, an army canteen cup which rests on the ground while he stands holding the shot glass full of whiskey at arm's length before him to drop it, he is adjudged "too drunk to mix his own," and others take over the task for him. Surprisingly, no serious casualties have resulted from these debauches, although Johnson and Hodges once wandered off and returned an hour later to find the rest of the boys decamped and had to walk twelve miles home.

The stag pow-wow serves the same function for the gang that the houseparty does for the fraternity. It is a jealously guarded tradition and has come to represent virility, carnival, and unique individuality. Its exploits of drunkenness become magnified into epics and are passing into legends. As in the case of the houseparty, pledges or new junior actives are always present in subordinate roles, and are thus presented with situations defined by their culture as "rewarding" and in which they can hope to participate as actors once their fraternity majority is attained.

The gang has two collective sports which are not shared with others in the fraternity. These are their trips "to the Monastery" and a further kind of nomadism they call "prowling and harassment."

"The Monastery" began in the collective life of the gang as the lake cottage owned by Fitzpatrick's parents. In the three years since its invention the term has come to mean any lake or river cottage to which they can retire for a vacation of drinking, fishing, hunting, and gambling. The boys refer to these trips as "withdrawals for rest, seclusion, and meditation," and insist on their definition as returns to nature from which they seek strength to deal with a crass and unfeeling world. (This formula was invented by MacKenzie who was interviewed after their first trip by a reporter from the school paper. When asked how he had spent his time during the vacation he replied, "In a damned monastery." Curiosity about this cryptic response led the gang to invent their ascetic explanation for their binges.) Although the term "monastery" has now come to stand for any cabin, THE Monastery remains Fitzpatrick's.

There may be some basis for MacKenzie's unexpectedly spiritual view of the gang's monastic trips, for the preferred time is late winter, when school has been in session for months and the winter season lies heavily on the northern landscape. Hodges and Lawrence in particular, in rare serious conversation, speak of their trips there as a means of "letting off steam" built up in the indoor months, of relaxing, and of "just fooling around for a change." Certainly nothing much happens on the typical trip. If their vacation is to be a weekend one, they usually skip school Friday afternoon, arriving at the cabin around dusk. Wood is chopped, fires started and food put on to cook, the pump thawed, and a meal of some kind is eaten by six. Cards and light drinking occupy the evening. The boys sleep late the following morning, arising only when hunger forces them from their sleeping bags. The remainder of Saturday is devoted to hunting in the surrounding woods, ice-fishing, target shooting, and "fooling around." Saturday night may see them once again drinking and playing cards in the cabin, or in attendance at some rural dance in a nearby farm community. Sunday morning is spent loafing and hunting or fishing and then the cabin is closed once more and the boys return to their homes for supper. They often attempt to find local girls who might be willing to return with them to the cabin for the night, but their search for sirens has thus far been unsuccessful.

Different from the trip to the monastery is the behavior the gang calls "prowling and harassment," which expresses hostility toward the adult world. The fraternity exists, for example, as an extralegal group in school and with the knowledge of school authorities with whom there is an unstated understanding that as long as the members behave while on school grounds the authorities will overlook the group's existence. Despite this mutually advantageous situation, the gang has adopted the harassment of teachers and principal as one of their informal goals. They upset the routines of the school day by rolling trash containers down the metal-shod stairs, by setting off fire alarms, by exploding firecrackers in the hall, and by other pranks. On one occasion MacKenzie locked a teacher in a classroom and on another Fitzpatrick and Johnson turned on a fire hose in a back hall where it ran for some time before discovery.

Fitzpatrick regularly foments fights in which the gang becomes involved, both with other school gangs and with strange groups on the downtown streets, and has even gone so far as to attack the city police department. Fitz and Johnson eagerly relate an incident when they threw tomatoes stolen from a sidewalk stand at a parked patrol car simply because "we tired of looking at the smug bastard's ugly face." When taken to police headquarters for a talk with juvenile authorities, they listened until suddenly queried, "Now who threw that tomato?" Said Fitzpatrick, "Do you mean tomahto?"

A similar situation is their persecution of a middle-aged citizen whom they believe to be a lawyer disbarred for malpractice. They call his home at all hours, making inquiries as, "Is this the West End Dog and Cat hospital?" or occasionally go to his door asking for "Mr. Simmons, the plumber." They have strewn his lawn with garbage and once planted a sign saying, "Shady Deals and Illegal Abortions Rendered Here," and always make it a point to dump their bottles on his front walk after a drunk. Their persistence in this persecution they explain by saying (1) that it is fun since the object of their attentions "always calls the cops and then comes out and tries to talk us into sticking around until they come" or (2) that it is simply "something to do."

On wheels the gang is a public menace because they observe the rules of the road scrupulously and force other drivers to do the same on threat of physical violence. Let someone crowd them from the lane, turn in front of them without signaling, or run a stop sign, and they are after him like minions of hell. Depending upon the circumstances (as what car they are driving, the age and sex of the other driver) they may crowd him into a lane of oncoming traffic, cut in front of him and force him to the curb to pick a fight, or simply tail him for miles blowing their horn and catcalling. Women are excused after being forced to listen to a lecture on auto etiquette. The most unfortunate offender of their private rule system is the impatient driver who blows his horn at any delay in starting after the change of traffic signals. When this offense occurs the gang may leap from their car and run back to the offender either demanding, on pain of violence, that he forthwith proceed to demonstrate each of his other accessories beside his horn, or even raise his hood and rip wires from sparkplugs, distributor, etc. The boys take great delight in these "applied lessons in driving courtesy," as they call them, and have only once run afoul of the law. Then they escaped before the officer, a foot patrolman, could apprehend them.

THE JOLLY ROGERS—COMMENTARY

The preceding description contains a number of points worth consideration. The boys involved are not what is popularly meant by "juvenile delinquents": young hoodlums or thugs. All but one are middle or upper class in their origins, and all are capable of considerable subordination to organizational requirements. In some respects they are juvenile "organization men." Some of their behaviors are explicable as adolescent high spirits and unrelieved energy, and by the gang's search for "something to do." There runs through them, however, a strand of hostility which cannot be so explained, for while it is exciting to contest with danger, many of their "harassing" actions seem calculated to be self-defeating. Attacking police cars, for example, can have only one outcome, while their guerrilla warfare in the school is bound, eventually, to end in their own defeat. Their hostility to the world of adults, whom they refer to as "the squares," is manifest in much they say and their insistence upon the letter of the law in the behavior of adults is also an expression of this outlook. The social functions of these conflicts are obvious. The gang members feel themselves to be, and physically are, adult. They are surrounded, however, by older people who treat them as children, and the war with the adult world in which they are engaged creates within the gang a strong social solidarity and identification between members, and a sense of belonging to a dramatic, accepting, and permissive group. Like that of any group, their cohesiveness increases with an external threat, so their social relations may be sufficient stimuli to provoke the behaviors discussed.

The boys' perpetual restlessness is more symptomatic of their underlying malaise than any other single behavior thus far noted. They are always on-the-go or fidgeting to be going.

They gather after school in a nearby delicatessen and ask each other, "Whaddawedo today?" Often the answer consists simply in piling into MacKenzie's car and going to some other part of town for chili and beer, or going downtown because someone needs to buy a comb. Wandering the downtown streets occupies many idle hours. Evenings may be spent bowling, at a movie, in a chili parlor playing pinball, or wandering aimlessly from one set of neon lights to another. If a sorority is meeting, an evening can be killed talking to the girls or playing the piano and singing. Mostly they do nothing—hang around a cafe or poolroom to talk, gossip, dream. Except as they create it, they are without status of any value to themselves; no longer children and not yet men, they can only wait, and occupy themselves as best they can. Consider the facts: (1) Most of the Jolly Rogers have no regular employment. The consequence is that they have no occupational associations to structure their behavior, no demands upon their time other than those made by their parents or their school. (2) Most of the boys have no steady girl friends or even avoid dating. To keep steady company with the opposite sex is to enter into a system of highly structured behavior expectations. Since the members of the Jolly Rogers do not have steady girls the modifying influence of such associations are absent for them. (3) Only three of the members of the group have *any* affiliations with school or community groups beside their fraternity. The boys live in social isolation (their fraternity aside), although none of them are "isolate" types. They have no group memberships or social contacts which could define their behavior through systematic patterns of expectation for them. They share meanings and values with no one of social significance to them. Since the adult world has no place for them and they are permitted to drift randomly in it, coming into conflict with it upon occasion, and unrewarded even when they do not, it is small wonder that they view it with suspicion and that their relations with it often take hostile forms.

It is probably this lack of status which explains the existence as well as the character of the gang. A status is a position in the world, a social location to which the individual belongs, providing him with expectations for his behavior that he must spend his time in fulfilling, and providing others with expectations about how he ought to fulfill them. Childhood is a status and adulthood has many, but for the young man with childhood behind and adult statuses not yet within reach, there is no place to go and nothing to do. He has nothing to do because he has no expectations to tell him how to act and other people have no expectations for him. The late teenager, therefore, exists in American society in a limbo of waiting and purposelessness. The fraternity and the gang are things to which the individual can give himself and that give him a place and a purpose, define things for him to do and be, and give him a reason for existing in a world otherwise without reason for him. That the Jolly Rogers are a fraternity instead of a delinquent gang is largely a matter of happenstance. If they came from other parts of the city they would be delinquent instead of restless and troublesome. As it is, the gang within the Jolly Rogers approaches delinquent status although all of its members (with t' e sole exception of Fitzpatrick) are from middle- or upper-class homes and most experience a reasonable degree of parental attention. Judging from the history of the fraternity most of its present members will go on to professional, technical, and managerial occupations in later life, and some will become "pillars of the community." It is an indictment of their community that it has failed to find any constructive use for their energies at the present time.[14]

Summary

This chapter has discussed disorganization of the social group. The three cases—beatniks, professional thieves, and the juvenile gang—are examples of both anomie and conflict. It is important to remember that this study is concerned with disorganization in *social relations* and that it is

[14] For what is probably the definitive study of gangs, the reader may wish to consult W. F. Whyte, *Street Corner Society*, 5th ed. (Chicago: University of Chicago Press, 1960).

quite possible for an organized group to participate in a disorganized situation. The professional thief and the juvenile gang member belong to highly organized groups and are often not themselves disorganized personalities. The groups to which they belong, however, are in conflict with other groups. In the case of the Beats, a relatively disorganized group composed in part of disorganized personalities, its relations are more anomic.

Conflict was defined as a situation where individuals in contact with one another shared a sufficient number of meanings and values to enable them to form social groups but in which the meanings and values peculiar to the groups were not shared with other groups. The cause of the Beats' disorganized state has been identified as consisting in their alienation from the dominant society in four senses. They are alienated in their belief in their *powerlessness* to affect their own fates, in the *meaninglessness* of their existences for themselves, in their *anomic* inability to accept common norms as effective means for the attainment of goals and, in their *isolation* from popular standards. The cause of the disorganization represented by the juvenile gang was identified as a lack of social statuses for teenagers in American society with a consequent absence of norms for their behavior. This, too, is a situation where anomie creates conflict.

The case of the professional criminal is less clear. The obvious cause of the disorganized condition is the criminal's adherence to a set of norms divergent from the usual ones acceptable to the larger society but this cannot explain the continued existence of such norms—of the underworld subculture. The problem (not dealt with here) of the causation of individual behavior—why certain individuals become alcoholics or criminals and others do not—is an entirely different one from the problem of the causation of the social phenomena with which this text is concerned. Such explanation is the province of the psychiatrist or social psychologist and as yet no theories entirely adequate to explain it have been propounded.

Chapter IV

THE DISORGANIZED ORGANIZATION

A scientific theory should have as broad a scope as possible. Thus far in this book the theory of social disorganization has been applied to individuals and to social groups. In this chapter the ideas are used in analysis of large-scale social organizations. This level of abstraction makes possible for the first time what might be called "organizational psycho-analysis," for not all of the behaviors examined in these pages are the products of conscious efforts by individuals. Some institutional patterns of behavior develop in a latent or "unconscious" manner in large-scale organizations, and though they may be necessary to the effective performance of the organization, they are brought forth by the social system without rational planning or awareness.

The three organizations discussed in the following pages—the university, the military establishment, and the mental hospital—disclose both anomie and conflict. In the typical case anomie is the product of divergent norms institutionalized in the organization (often as a result of incompatibilities between its goals and the unintended consequences of its means for achieving them) and conflict between organizational groups may be the consequence of that anomie or may support the norms producing it. Sometimes the organization has a set of mutually inconsistent goals; in other cases the means it has developed for achieving its goals may be in some manner incompatible with the goals themselves. In such situations the effect on the organization may be to reduce its efficiency and to create strife between its members while subjecting them to agonizing personal frustrations and anxieties.

The American University[1]

The reader is probably aware of the crises which face higher education. The "tidal wave" of expected college enrollment has already hit the colleges and universities, as the bumper baby crop of the early 1940's has come to college age and it is causing severe stresses. This boom in students has been accelerated by an increasing tendency on the part of the American college-age population to go to college, so that greater proportions of each generation matriculate in an institution of higher education than did in the generation preceding them.

The Second World War, as is well known, gave the fundamental impetus to this situation. American colleges and universities experienced a tremendous expansion immediately after it in terms of students, functions, activities, and plants. Further, the demands of the war and the enrollment wave of veterans afterward precipitated radical changes in the organization and ideologies of the university and the academic profession. For the first time in recent history the universities experienced a real demand for the services they had to offer. There was a time in 1942 when it became exigently necessary for many people concerned with the operation of the war to know something about the tides at an insignificant island named Betio in the atoll of Tarawa; later the effect of individual "rotation" upon the combat efficiency of units became of pressing importance; and still later the peculiar and esoteric behaviors of the particles in the subatomic world were of extravagant concern. Knowledge—as *knowledge*—for the first time in American history became a commodity in general demand. And the only source for thousands of such essential pieces of information lay in the minds and the laboratories of the colleges and universities of America and the United Kingdom.

The practical utility of academic knowledge having been

[1] This section is in part based on the author's work with Theodore Caplow reported in *The Academic Marketplace* (New York: Basic Books Inc., 1958), copyright © 1958, Basic Books Inc. Used with permission of the publisher.

established by the demands of the Second World War, business and industry set about utilizing it after the war. Between the requirements of war and the later requirements of peace, a readjustment was experienced by American universities in 1942-1947 and is still going on. Industry experienced a similar wartime crisis—"the managerial crisis"—and survived it by transforming its assumptions, procedures, and policies. Similar transformations have not yet taken place in the universities, but will have to occur in the immediate future. It is obviously impossible to double faculties and physical plants in order to meet the doubled enrollments expected within the next decade. The alleviations which have been suggested—teaching via television, the twelve-hour day, the six-day week, among others—are only expedients and will not *solve* the problem. There are already a number of strains in the system of higher education imposed by increasing enrollments. These have exposed not only the obvious faults and problems in the present structure, but others heretofore largely hidden from view. Some result from the structure of the academic profession and qualify as instances of social disorganization. We shall discuss only two of these: professional orientations and institutional lawlessness.

These observations about American universities are based upon data gathered in 1957 by the Faculty Mobility Study directed by Theodore Caplow, then at the University of Minnesota, and sponsored by the Fund for the Advancement of Education. The Study began as an inquiry into the problem of faculty "turnover" in universities, but grew into an analysis and critique of major segments of the institution of higher education. Ten American universities, chosen to represent a wide range of characteristics, were studied. They may not be identified, for interviews in them were conducted under the assurance of confidence, but they may be described: Three are Ivy League, four are Big Ten, one is on the Pacific Coast, two are in the South. Five are endowed (privately supported) and five are state supported. Five are metropolitan universities, two are located in middle-sized cities, and three are in small college towns. Three have degree-granting branches, five have more than one liberal-arts college, and two have separate colleges for men and for women. They are all *major* institutions; together they account for over one-third of all nonmedical doctorates awarded annually in the United States.

The technique of the study was to secure from the deans of the colleges of liberal arts lists of all vacancies created in a two-year period by the departures, retirements, or deaths of men in the ranks of assistant, associate, or full professor. Armed with these lists, interviewers approached the chairman and colleagues of each departed man and conducted an hour-long interview about the reasons for his departure, the departmental search for a replacement, and the reasons why the department selected the particular replacement it did. In all, 215 faculty vacancies were studied through interviews with over 400 persons from instructors to university presidents.

It is important to observe one caution in assessing the conclusions of the study: that they are applicable only in the world of the *major league* universities. The professors in the great universities of the United States habitually define higher education as consisting of institutions at three levels of size and quality. These are often referred to in baseball terms: the expression "major league" means institutions such as those which constitute the Ivy League and the Big Ten, "minor league" refers to the other state universities and the better private universities and colleges, and "bush league" refers to the host of state colleges, teachers' colleges, junior colleges, and so on, not included in the first two categories. The minor- and bush-league social systems are quite different from those of the major universities, and such institutions may be expected to have quite different sets of problems. The discussion, therefore, concerns only the world of major universities.

UNIVERSITY ORGANIZATION—SOME DEFINITIONS AND PERSPECTIVES

A university is a cluster of relatively independent colleges, each headed by a dean responsible only to the presi-

●   105

dent of the university or his executive officer for its operation. Most colleges are subdivided into departments. The department, headed by a chairman, is the fundamental unit of academic affiliation, and is usually the institutional embodiment of an academic discipline. The department is called the "fundamental unit" of affiliation because faculty members tend to identify themselves with their departments and form emotional attachments to them. The department, further, is the basic budgeting unit of the university. It is usually conceived by its members as a task-performing group, although it has no group task beyond the highly generalized one of "teaching English" (or sociology, or chemistry, or whatever).

Another concept important to comprehension of the nature of the university is the academic discipline. The term usually refers to (1) a body of subject matter, (2) the men who practice or teach the subject, and (3) the professional organizations and activities of those men.

The organization of the discipline usually found within the liberal-arts college may be described by reference to sociology. Similar kinds of activities and relations are found in most of the other arts-college disciplines, although the numbers and magnitudes involved differ somewhat with the different disciplines. In the United States there are perhaps 10,000 to 15,000 individuals who might be called "sociologists" in that they either practice the activities known as sociology or teach at least one course in that subject. Of this estimated number, approximately 7,000 are dues-paying members of the American Sociological Association, the professional organization of sociologists comparable to the American Medical Association for physicians. Within these 7,000 members of the A.S.A., there is a core largely composed of research scholars and numbering perhaps no more than 500 men. In a very real sense these individuals *are* American sociology. These are the men who write textbooks, fill journals with articles, man committees of the Association, are called upon by the federal government for consultation and technical advice, sit on committees of fund-granting foundations to determine who will or will not receive financial support for his work, fill professorial chairs in sociology at the major universities, and, by their activities and their judgments, define what the discipline of sociology is, does and ought to be and do.

This organized and specialized discipline is a relatively new development on the academic scene. Not long ago one professor in his thirty-seven years at a northern university taught classes in chemistry, physics, mathematics, zoology, geology, logic, mineralogy, botany, and Greek. That is, a professor was once a teacher; today he is usually a teacher *of something* and is occasionally not a teacher at all, for there are some few men with academic appointments for full-time research activities.

PROFESSIONAL ORIENTATIONS

For the contemporary American professor his discipline consists of a body of content and methods and of a set of attitudes or viewpoints toward either or both, plus a set of attitudes about other disciplines.

Again a simplified description of sociology may be used for illustrative purposes. Assume that Assistant Professor X is a young, recently graduated doctor of philosophy from one of the major universities of the country. With regard to his views about the content of sociology, he is apt to be classifiable either as a social psychologist or as a student of social organizations and institutions. With regard to the methods he will use in his research, he is apt to be classifiable either as a "statistician" or as a "theorist." With regard to his viewpoints about his field, he is apt to be either a statistical or a theoretical social psychologist or a statistical or a theoretical student of social organization and institutions; no other viewpoints are possible, or, at least, no others can guarantee him the possibility of professional success in his chosen field. With regard to his attitude toward other disciplines, and varying somewhat with his views about the content and methods of his own, he is likely to favorably regard the natural sciences, anthropology, experimental psychology, history, and perhaps

●   107

economics. He is likely to disdain education, social work, and psychoanalysis.

The importance of viewpoints of this kind varies. They tend to be least important in the objective disciplines of the natural sciences, and to be most important in the subjective disciplines of the humanities. One of the consequences of this fact is that men in the objective fields are regarded much like the working parts of machinery, each one being potentially replaceable by another of essentially identical quality, training, and competence, whereas in the more subjective fields individuals are regarded as unique.

There are organizational consequences of the importance or nonimportance of viewpoints as well. One of these is the possibility of "owning" courses. In departments of physics in major universities it is common for professors to rotate teaching of the standard undergraduate courses. In the humanities, on the other hand, men are identified with specialties which they and only they are deemed capable of teaching. The "Shakespeare man" in the English Department may lend "his" courses to another while he goes on sabbatical leave, but they are still "his" and when he returns he will expect them back.

A second such consequence is the ease with which men are evaluated or assessed. In physics, if the department is looking for a specialist in cosmic rays, almost any man with a recent doctor's degree from Minnesota, Carnegie Tech, M.I.T., or Cal Tech will do, because the fact that the individual has a recent degree with such a specialty from one of these institutions is itself sufficient to indicate his competence. In the more subjective fields, on the other hand, it may prove practically impossible to assess an individual's competence since the viewpoints keep getting in the way.

A third such consequence is the "guild" aspect of certain disciplines. Physicists, within their vocational specialties, and mathematicians, are fond of describing their disciplines as "guilds." In a real sense they are guilds. Cosmic-ray or nuclear physicists and members of the American Mathematical Society generally know everyone else in their area, correspond with large numbers of people, talk to each other over the long-distance telephone, frequently travel to conventions where they see each other and exchange gossip. One respondent from a mathematics department remarked that when he traveled across the country he seldom had to pay a hotel bill, since he was expected to stay with professional friends.

Perhaps the most important of these organizational consequences of the existence of viewpoints in the disciplines is that of the "disciplinary orientation" versus the "institutional orientation." This is a matter of an older ethic as well as a matter of viewpoints, and one evident social problem in the academic profession results from these conflicting orientations. To the extent that a man is directed toward the professional activities of his discipline, he is apt to be directed away from his institution, and vice versa. The reason is that many of the activities constituting the disciplinary orientation make it impossible to perform institutionally oriented activities. Discipline-oriented men, for example, do laboratory or field or library research, publish findings in the form of scholarly books and articles, travel to professional convocations and conventions, circulate among the great departments, visit colleagues active in their specialties, concentrate their teaching efforts at the graduate level. These activities inevitably mean that they are away from their institutions a great deal and have relatively few contacts with people in the community in which it is located or with undergraduate students. The institutional orientation, on the other hand, demands that the professor spend much of his time teaching undergraduate classes, serving on institutional committees, engaging in public-service activities in the city or state in which his university is located, and generally "staying put." If a professor is in London at a professional convention, he cannot be in his office for undergraduate consultation. If he is in his laboratory he cannot simultaneously be teaching large numbers of undergraduates the ABC's of introductory psychology. If he is addressing the local Chamber of Commerce on the latest developments in automation, he cannot at the same time address a convocation of learned colleagues. Consequently men often have to choose early in their careers whether to make their ways primarily in their disciplines or in their institutions. In the major universities the choice usually goes to the discipline and the professor identifies himself as a physicist, psychologist, or speech therapist, and not as a professor at State University.

A fundamental contradiction is thus *built into* the role of the university professor in America today. The functions of the university undeniably include the creation of knowledge through research and scholarship but, on the other hand, even in privately endowed institutions teaching is also supposed to be a part of the academic job. Few universities would remain in existence if they stopped teaching. Yet for a man to acquire eminence in his discipline he must to a great extent ignore teaching and concentrate upon research activities. The universities compound this tension by accepting the disciplinary criteria of quality, and firing men who do not measure up to the standards of competence set by their disciplines.[2]

Institutional Lawlessness[3]

It is a little-recognized fact that universities are relatively lawless organizations in some respects. The professor may object to this characterization and protest that trivialities of procedures are a source of constant harassment, but such regulation is conspicuously absent in one area of great significance in the university: personnel policy and relationships and in particular the authority structure of the university as it is related to these. It is here that universities, although they are bureaucracies and have many resemblances to military and industrial structures, differ radically and significantly from them.

[2] For some recent reactions to this situation, see Jacques Barzun, *The House of Intellect* (New York: Harper and Brothers, 1959) and "The Cult of Research and Creativity," *Harper's Magazine*, 221:1325, October, 1960.

[3] The following section, based on the previously cited research, was originally reported by the author in "Limitations on Communication in Large-Scale Organizations," *Proceedings* of the Annual Meeting of the Midwest Sociological Society, April, 1958.

In an industrial or a military bureaucracy the power to bestow merit lies in the same hands which hold the power to assign seniority through promotion and salary. Thus the two orders of merit and seniority are seldom permitted to get far out of adjustment. To use a military analogy no captain may ever be allowed for long to be significantly superior in professional performance to any major, and if his performance has been outstanding, a way will be made to promote him. Similarly, a major whose seniority demands that he receive promotion, while his merit is not sufficient to warrant it, will either be removed from the organization or will be allotted the necessary merit. There are devices, such as the Legion of Merit, which have exactly this as one of their functions, if not purposes.

This correlation is not possible in the university because, while seniority is controlled by the institution, and awarded through institutional procedures, merit is not. The professional merit of the academic man is largely measured and awarded through the evaluations of other members of his discipline and the university exercises no control over it.

If a university, like a corporation or an army, were to assign large areas of specific power-over-persons to particular positions, it would be possible for the incumbent of one of those positions, say a dean, to have power, by virtue of seniority, over other individuals who were clearly *his* seniors in professional merit. This power would be intolerable because it would make professional prestige meaningless, and might destroy the organization because of personnel difficulties arising from that fact. But one requirement which any large-scale organization has for the successful fulfillment of its functions is that a great deal of power must be exercised in it; decisions must be made and men must be made to carry out those decisions. The solution to this dilemma in American universities has been to let power lodge where it may, to let it "roll free" to be taken into whatever hands are capable of exercising it, and to permit situations to "decide themselves" in the absence of specific rules for the attachment of authority to particular positions.

In this sense universities are lawless organizations: there

are few rules for the establishment of power or the exercise of power by individuals in particular positions. One result is that a great deal of arbitrary and often capricious power may be assembled and wielded by persons without any institutional responsibility for it: witness the "robber baron" chairman or dean and the professor from whom the president must seek acquiescence in any plans if those plans are to succeed. Another result is that the institution itself, rather than operating in rational order for the accomplishment of its goals, moves by fits and starts in many directions in a kind of evolutionary anarchy.

The major consequence for the university of the problems discussed above has been the progressive dislocation of its undergraduate instruction and its progressive fragmentation into a thousand splintered empires as men seek to establish and control their fortunes for themselves in the absence of rules. "No educational experiment ever fails," is an old cliché of the faculty clubs.

The "disorganized" nature of the university is in part created by the fact that its functions are threefold and not unitary. The university *is* a university because it creates, conserves, and disseminates knowledge. In the United States, and especially in state-supported institutions, the disseminative function, carried on through undergraduate instruction, has always been of great if not paramount importance. The increasing enrollment of the next decades will stress this function more than ever. It will strike the universities, however, at a time when they are more than ever directing themselves to other functions, particularly to their mandate for research. It is right that they should have that mandate for there are no other institutions in American society, except a few government-sponsored physical laboratories, in which the pure and undirected search for knowledge *as* knowledge is carried on.

As in other cases to be examined, the stresses and problems of the university are actually *built into* its present organization. Given the nature and history of the American university they are inevitable. But these stresses will be unsupportable in the near future unless some radically new means of effecting the university's functions are invented. Given the levels of financial support the American public seems willing to provide for higher education, and given the pressure on it that the enrollments of students already in the high schools will provide, new means of accomplishing the old functions seem essential. They have not yet been invented, or, if they have, they have remained untried.

The Military Academy and Military Life[4]

The function of a military academy is to make professional officers from civilians or enlisted men. This objective is primarily accomplished by a twofold process: (1) the transmission of technical knowledge, and (2) the installation of an appropriate professional outlook or frame of reference. At present in the military Academies of the United States, the transmission of technical knowledge has largely been superseded by the indoctrination function, for all the services maintain extensive educational institutions and programs for teaching their highly specialized knowledge to both officer and enlisted personnel. While some basic technical information is still imparted by the academies, the body of technical "know-how" necessary to the operation of a modern military force is largely instilled in service schools such as the Infantry School, the Artillery School, and the Staff College. Indoctrination in the professional viewpoint, which remains the Academies' primary job, is accomplished by suppressing pre-existing statuses, by teaching new rules and requiring adjustment to conflict between rules, by treatment calculated to develop solidarity, and by stimulating the assumption of upper-class status.

[4] The following section on the social functions of the military academy is in part based on the author's experiences as a cadet, but comes largely from an article by S. M. Dornbusch, "The Military Academy as an Assimilating Institution," *Social Forces*, 33:4, May, 1955. Copyright © 1955 by the Williams and Wilkins Company. Used with the permission of the author and the publisher.

SUPPRESSION OF PRE-EXISTING STATUSES

The new cadet or plebe at the military Academy is by definition the lowest of all life forms. At West Point, for example, the plebe reports in the early summer for a period of intensive indoctrination, basic training, and hazing known as "Beast Barracks." He is usually met by upper classmen as he climbs off the bus to report to school, and is immediately shouted into ranks with other new arrivals and marched off by overbearing upper classmen to acquire a haircut and a new uniform. This period of intense hazing lasts through most of the summer, and is primarily designed to fix his low status in the mind of the new cadet. The assignment of this low status encourages the plebe to place a high value upon successful completion of his Academy career, and, additionally, requires that he lose all identifications with pre-existing civilian statuses. This clean break with the past must be accomplished in a relatively short period. For this reason the plebe is not allowed to leave the grounds of the academy or engage in social intercourse with noncadets.

The new cadet's complete dependence upon the academy social system is repeatedly demonstrated to him in many ways, for example the demerit system. Infractions of regulations are punished by the assignment of "demerits" to cadets. In order for the cadet to be promoted or even maintained at the Academy, demerits must be worked off through fatigue details or marched off on punishment rounds. It is not uncommon for plebes to be "ripped" by upper classmen (that is, assigned demerits) for no particular offense and be told, "That's for nothing, now do something." This authoritarian and arbitrary system of discipline tends to produce in a short time a homogeneous group of plebes from a heterogeneous collection of persons of widely variant statuses and backgrounds.

Other practices reinforce the process: uniforms are always issued to a new plebe class as soon as possible, usually on the first day, and "G.I." haircuts are given at the same time.

The immediate putting on of the uniform and the regulation haircut remove civilian status symbols. The poor boy who arrives in blue jeans and a worn sportshirt and the rich boy who arrives in Harris Tweeds are soon indistinguishable in outward appearance. At one of the Academies it was once the practice to forbid the wearing of any personal jewelry except wrist watches, and even these had to have plain leather straps of uniform color. Discussion of wealth, family, and background is strictly taboo so that invidious comparisons between civilian statuses may not be made. Cadet pay is low, but cadets are not permitted to receive money from home so that the possession of different amounts of spending money cannot distinguish them. The plebe's role as a cadet must supersede all other accustomed roles, and no objective clues are left to reveal his outside status.

Learning New Rules and Adjusting to Conflicts between Rules

There are two sets of rules governing cadet behavior:

(1) *The Regulations of the Academy* (usually believed by outsiders to be the primary source of control over cadets). These are similar to the ethical code of any profession or to the Army Regulations or the Regulations for the Government of the Navy. They serve, in part, as propaganda for outsiders, but additionally they support a second set of expectations.

(2) *The Informal Rules.* Offenses against informal rules are usually defined as breaches of the formal code, and appropriate punishments are applied. This punitive system tends to conceal the existence of the informal rules. For example, hazing of plebes by upper classmen is officially prohibited at all Academies. But when a plebe refuses to submit to hazing on the grounds that the formal regulations prohibit it, he will be charged for "insubordination" and find himself walking punishment rounds or painting walls. His offense appears in the Academy books as an offense against the formal regula-

●   115

tions, and the breach of tradition involved in his refusal to submit to hazing is never brought to light. In cases of conflict between the formal regulations and the informal rules or traditions, the regulations are usually superseded by the traditions. For example, it is against regulations at all Academies for cadets to have food in their rooms. It is common practice, however, for first classmen to order plebes to bring them candy or other food from the Academy canteen or ship's service. If the food-carrying plebe is caught in the cadet barracks with food in his hand by another upper classman, following tradition he will offer no excuse for his behavior and receive a stiff dose of demerits. Since the plebe is not to blame for his offense, the upper classman who ordered the food will then inform his classmates that they are to withhold further demerits from that plebe until he has been excused from offenses meriting the number applied when he was caught. In effect the plebe is given license to commit offenses worth that many demerits. Thus Academy experience teaches future officers that the formal regulations of their services are not paramount when they conflict with the informal behavior codes of the officer corps.

As might be expected, the plebe class frequently develops feelings of persecution and rebellion as a result of such discipline. Since frustrations demand outlets, some infractions are traditionally allowed the plebe class. At one Academy these include climbing the water tower to steal the bulb from the aircraft warning light on top of it, and stealing food from the mess hall. The plebe who allows himself to be caught brazenly in one of these acts will probably be "ripped" for it, but as long as he takes reasonable precautions an upper classman accidentally coming upon the scene is likely to look the other way.

DEVELOPMENT OF SOLIDARITY

Social control in the military Academies operates through the class hierarchy. The first class, the seniors, are only nominally under the control of the commissioned officers on duty at the institution. Few Academy officials check their activities, so minor regulations may be broken with impunity. The first class, in turn, is given almost total control over the rest of the cadet corps. The second and third classes—the juniors and sophomores—haze the plebes, a practice forbidden by regulations but hallowed by centuries of tradition at Annapolis and West Point. Since the first classmen demand the hazing and they give demerits to lower classmen, the lower classes follow suit. As a consequence of undergoing hazing together, the successive plebe classes tend to develop a remarkable social solidarity. For example, when an instructor calls upon a plebe in class, if he cannot answer the question and the instructor then asks it of other class members, the others all insist that they too are ignorant of the answer, in order to avoid the appearance of "showing up" their classmate. This intraclass cohesion persists throughout the academy and beyond: first classmen "rip" one another only on direct order of a commissioned officer, and in later years if a classmate behaves incompetently in battle he may be promoted, given the Legion of Merit, and returned to the United States instead of being shot or dishonorably discharged as might occur in some forces.

The basis for interclass solidarity (the development of a unified group feeling throughout the entire cadet corps) is not so obvious. Primarily, it develops through informal contacts between members of the different classes. The upper classmen who haze the plebes usually live in the same buildings with them, and, coming from a culture where aggressive authoritarianism is strongly disapproved, they feel guilty about their behavior and often visit the plebes informally to explain their disciplinary actions and to correct mistakes. Most upper classmen really wish to be known as good fellows to their subordinates, and, while they will be hard on parade, they may make sure that the man they ripped and put "in hock" for a week has a malted milk smuggled to him at night from the Academy canteen. Knowledge of common interests and destiny cannot be overlooked as an additional unifying force for the development of interclass solidarity. This is expressed through identification of the interests of individual cadets with those of the service to which they belong. A large appropriation for that service hastens the promotion of all officers in it; winning Academy football teams familiarize the civilian world with their alma mater; and good publicity for their service tends to raise the status of its entire officer corps.

Another basis for solidarity within the cadet and officer corps of the services is the manner in which "regulars" are united in their disdain for reservists. This unity is in part a result of the American custom (prior to World War II) of treating professional soldiers as the approximate social equals of men on relief and of budgeting the services accordingly. (There were times in the pacification of the West after the Civil War when regular Army officers who had commanded regiments or brigades as colonels or generals during the war had to buy supplies for their campaigns with borrowed money which they paid back at high rates of interest from their lieutenant's or captain's salaries.) The disdain is probably also a result of the fact that before World War II only a few reservists shared the privations of peacetime service with regulars, while the status of the regulars was swamped by them in war. And though reservists are seldom permitted to achieve the higher ranks in the American services, they are a threat to cadets and to recent Academy graduates. Reserve officers receive, through college ROTC programs or short correspondence or officers-candidate courses, the same ranks and salaries that regular officers acquire after four arduous years of Academy training. The Academy men, therefore, represent reservists as incompetents. When a cadet falters on parade, he is told, "You march like a reservist." Cadets are told to behave themselves on pass for "How else will people know that they are not reservists?" And myths are elaborated elevating the status of the regular at the expense of the re-servist. (A common wartime Army myth tells of the reserve colonel in command of a regiment in battle who has to call upon his regular lieutenants for tactical advice.) All of these behaviors assure the regulars that although the interlopers are allowed to have the same ranks, they may never share the status and prestige of the regular.

As the cadet increasingly identifies with his role of professional soldier, an increase in self-esteem accompanies the identification. Cadets are told again and again that they are members of an elite group which is necessary to and respected by the community, and they begin to feel at ease in superordinate roles: although they may be junior members of the cadet corps, the corps itself has high prestige. The degree to which the new role displaces the old is indicated by the fact that when cadets return to their homes for the first time after entering the Academies—normally the Christmas leave— they often experience conflicts between their new roles as cadets and the roles to which their parents and families are accustomed. The usual gossip in the cadet barracks after the leave is how much things at home have changed. That these estimations of superiority develop self-confidence in men otherwise lacking it is especially shown in connection with dating behavior. It is immensely satisfying to the self-esteem of the cadet when he realizes that he can get a date any time he wishes simply because he is a cadet.

Assumption of Upper-Class Status

Most cadets are drawn from middle-class backgrounds. They are seldom members of any aristocracy of wealth or breeding and hence are unused to defining themselves as members of an elite. From the time they arrive at the Academy, cadets are drilled in the idea that they will be members of a social elite in their later careers, and therefore obstacles they meet in their training and in the Academy social system become defined as those to be expected in the path of the upwardly mobile and as challenges to be surmounted. Certain Academy practices strongly reinforce this belief that cadets are there in part to learn to be members of an upper class. In all the Academies there is strong emphasis on etiquette, from the proper use of the calling card to table manners. (Reserve members of the officer corps often find military customs relating to calling on the commanding officer, leaving calling cards, and other social conduct incomprehensible and archaic.)

At most of the Academies cadets must submit for approval by the Academy staff the names of girls whom they wish to escort to Academy functions. Usually any girls attending nearby upper-class colleges are automatically eligible, while working girls from nearby towns are automatically taboo. There are sometimes further traditions which encourage forced associations with upper-class girls. A common one is that after the initial period of isolation of the plebe class, plebes may be required to attend an Academy dance where all of the girls present are relatives or friends of the officers serving at the Academy. At one Academy it was the custom for the cadet corps to be told at 6:30 P.M. that they were going to attend a dance given by the student body of a nearby upper-class girls' college, whereupon the cadets would be ordered into dress uniform, loaded on buses and trucks, and sent, under guard, to the campus of the girls' school. A week or two later the commanding officer of the Academy would inform the assembled cadet corps that they were to sponsor a return invitation dance, and the girls would be imported—under somewhat more favorable conditions of transport—in the same way. In these ways even the cadet's acquaintances with girls put him in contact with agents reinforcing his new social role.

Justification of Institutional Practices

In addition to the social mobility theme which views the rigors of Academy life as surmountable obstacles to the attainment of high social status, there are more open methods of legitimating traditional practices. The discipline is defended as a technique for identifying the weak and the incompetent or the undisciplined, and the cadet who rebels or resigns is defined as lacking character and his act is defined as an admission of defeat. "Separating the men from the boys" thus redefines the harsh traditions of the Academy into tests of the individual's ability to survive stress. The result of this definition of resignation is that most resignations take place only after the initial period of intensive hazing lets up so that, from the point of view of the resigning cadet, his behavior cannot be seen as an admission of his inability to "take it." Cadet resignations are viewed as threats to the morale of the entire cadet corps and those in the process of resignation are usually isolated from other cadets and excused from duties and classes in order to protect others from their disenchantment.

In these ways service Academies prepare future professional military officers for a demanding social role by isolating them from civilian society while offering them new roles and values and changing their self-conceptions in order to fit the behavior patterns manifested in and demanded by a unique occupation. As we have seen, however, the Academies also build permanent strains or tensions into the profession in the accomplishment of these functions. The most obvious of these—to civilian eyes—are those supporting traditions over law and regulations, and the strong class solidarity of Academy graduates. The "West Point and Annapolis Protective Associations" are familiar features of politics and of military policy in the United States.

The exigencies of the cold war and the necessity for a permanent military establishment of 2½ million men have reduced some of the old stresses between regulars and reservists, but they still haunt the careers of officers without Academy ties, and have often worked considerable hardship upon them. (In recent years many officers with reserve commissions and fifteen to nineteen years of service, sometimes with ranks as high as colonel, have been offered the choice between dismissal from the service or resignation of their commissions and enlistment in noncommissioned grades for the remainder of their service before retirement.) The reservist also creates a strain in the status of the regular. All military institutions in part derive from medieval traditions, one of which is that the officer corps is drawn from the aristocratic classes. This tradition still holds in some degree for all European armies except the Russian, and the military institutions of the United States have inherited the traditions without inheriting the aristocracy to support them. The United States officer corps, therefore, has had to justify its privileges on the rationalization that it is an aristocracy of training if not of birth. But reservists in the officer corps call even this rationalization into question, for they share the same ranks without formal Academy training and since World War II have proved indispensable to the system. The military have met this situation by giving the *regular commission* a higher status and by granting it to the reservist as a reward for competence and symbol of permanency. Yet the insistent demands both of a peacetime economy and a giant military establishment have meant that increasingly Academy gradu-ates leave the service while those who remain are forced to compete on more equal terms with officers commissioned in the ROTC and the National Guard who may come from higher social strata than their own. The way in which this conflict in status works out for the individual can only be imagined since there are no data on it, but it must often involve acute social and emotional problems exacerbated by the low prestige in which military life is held in American society. The ways in which it affects the social structure of the military establishment itself have been studied by Arnold Rose.

THE SOCIAL STRUCTURE OF THE ARMY[5]

The social structure of the United States Army is determined by the interaction of three traditions: (1) *the modern American tradition* of efficiency, self-interest, and individualism, (2) *the medieval or feudal tradition* of rigid separation of castes, hierarchical control, absence of moral accountability for the upper strata, and the assessment of the

[5] The following discussion is based on the article "The Social Structure of the Army," by Arnold Rose, *American Journal of Sociology*, li:5, March, 1946, copyright 1946, The University of Chicago Press. Used with the per-mission of the author and the publisher.

privileges of the lower strata as devices by which the members of the upper may manipulate them, (3) *the changing body of military doctrine* found in the laws describing the operation of the Army—the Army Regulations. The Regulations theoretically govern the Army but its social structure is set by the feudal tradition.

Of these three governing traditions the medieval is the strongest, but the Army has been modified by infusions of men with civilian attitudes and by the growth within it of new organizations such as the Air Force (now a separate service). Medievalism is still pre-eminent whenever conflicts between it and the Regulations occur, and it also tends to be stronger than the modern American tradition; witness the way in which civilian standards, especially of efficiency, are abandoned for the "Army way." But although medievalism still tends to dominate the Army's social structure, each of the three traditions operates under conditions and with modifications set by the other two. For example, Americans regard the feudal-medieval system as an evil and exploitive form of social structure, ignoring the fact that the statuses involved had *mutual* obligations and responsibilities; the welfare of his serfs was the obligation of the lord, and, in his own fashion, he fulfilled it. The German army developed the feudal tradition of the responsibility of the officer for his subordinates to a high degree and, before the destruction of the Wehrmacht in battle, good officer-enlisted relations were the keystone of its high morale. The United States Army has discarded the medieval paternalism but has developed no effective substitute for it.

The American tradition leads to the recognition in the Army Regulations that each soldier is an individual with rights and interests of his own and to the attempt to adapt the individual to his military occupation through such devices as the General Classification Test. But the American tradition also tends to stress "looking out for Number One" (rugged individualism), and officers are in a better position to look out for themselves than are enlisted men. The medieval tradition reinforces this advantage by not holding the officer morally accountable to his subordinates, yet it conflicts with the American tradition of individualism by insisting that he is *physically* responsible for them. Thus the American tradition tends both to operate against feudalism and simultaneously to operate against the Regulations to impose it.

The Army Regulations in part preserve medieval paternalism by stressing that the officer should look out for his men, not eating until they have eaten, and otherwise be responsible for them, but in practice the strength of the individualistic American tradition all but abolishes this stress. But under the Regulations enlisted men are for all practical purposes without recourse beyond their commanding officer and if he exploits them they are effectively helpless. They tend, therefore, to develop an informal "underground" in strong peer groups for self-protective purposes.[6]

INFORMAL STATUS RELATIONS IN THE ARMY[7]

There are three major status groupings in a military unit: superiors, equals, and inferiors.

Superiors. Superiors are systematically ignorant of inferiors, and even if the superiors were to seek information it would probably be unobtainable for lack of channels by which they could obtain knowledge. The reasons for this state of affairs may be found in the nature of military organization. The structure and its demands upon the superior make the inferior an object of interest only in a service- or task-performing capacity, which determines the only precise information the superior possesses about him: his occupational capabilities.

[6] For an excellent discussion of some more complicated technical and professional problems besetting the American military at the present time see Morris Janowitz, *The Professional Soldier* (Glencoe, Ill.: The Free Press, 1960), especially the chapters dealing with the "heroic" and "managerial" professional roles and the "pragmatic" and "absolutist" frames of reference or viewpoints about the functions of modern war.

[7] This discussion is based primarily upon the author's long participant observation of the Army of the United States.

The missing information would probably be impossible to obtain because the status hierarchy is so constituted that it is difficult for a superior to observe an inferior, to elicit information from or about him, or to "get to him" in any way if the inferior does not permit him to do so. For example, it is impossible in either of two possible situations for a superior to observe an inferior at work in the military context: (1) In a situation where the inferior has his own inferiors in charge, he can simply stand aside and permit the observing superior of higher rank to act as overseer for him. (2) Should the observed individual be of the lowest rank and have no inferiors of his own, the superior cannot observe him at work for any length of time for to do so is to demean his own status into that of a "bird dog" as well as to usurp the rightful position of another, the intermediate inferior, if he is present. Likewise it is difficult to observe an inferior in his quarters because the presence of a superior makes peer-group operation impossible and little activity will occur. Similarly a superior cannot observe inferiors at play, for superiors are not allowed to play where their inferiors play, and, should a superior chance upon the scene, all play ceases. There are few other avenues open to the superior who desires information about his inferiors. Eavesdropping is unthinkable and the results of it would be of severely limited application. Direct interrogation is even more futile. There is no recourse from "I do not understand you, sir," or "I do not know . . . I was not there . . . I have not heard . . ." In certain circumstances, the use of informants from the inferior group is satisfactory, but it has serious limitations. The risk of becoming compromised is always present, the reliability of the informant may never be known, and he is always marginal (for what in-group tolerates an informer?). Further, once committed to action on his information, the superior has in effect placed himself under the influence of the informer.

In summary, the superior neither needs nor usually wants information about his inferiors other than what the system provides him. In case he does wish more, he is unlikely to get it.

Equals. Aside from certain information about his superiors, as suggested below, the knowledge most necessary to an individual in the military context is knowledge about his equals and the status group which includes them all. Again, the reason for this paramount need may be discovered through reference to the hierarchical organization. The peer group acts as a mutual protective and beneficial society for its members, shielding them from a powerful and sometimes unpredictable system, and assisting them in the performance of their duties and in the attainment of rewards and satisfactions. Gossip, the transfer of information, furthers these functions; the peer group is a talking group. To maximize its performance a high order of knowledge about one another is necessary, for the group must act under pressure and maintain a tight-knit solidarity against nonmembers. Informing is not tolerated, for example, nor is striving nor currying favor. In threatening situations the group must present a united front with every individual acting like every other. Such unity of behavior may be obtained only through intimate knowledge of each others' opinions and behaviors.

Inferiors. Superiors are of considerable interest to inferiors, and inferiors have access to channels through which they can inform themselves and expand that interest. Should an inferior wish to scrutinize the life of his superior within the military context, it is almost impossible for the superior to escape him. Again, the reasons for the inferior's interest and his ability to satisfy it lie with the nature of the organization.

The inferior in the military caste system is in some respects totally at the mercy of his superior. In this uncomfortable position he has only two means for protecting himself: (1) his peer group, the efficacy of which depends in large part upon specific and external factors over which he has no control; and (2) his knowledge of, and consequent ability to predict and adapt to, the behavior of his superiors. The usefulness of this knowledge explains the inferior's effort to learn intimate details about the personality of his superior and the inferior's avid interest in receiving new information about him and his behavior.

The dimensions of knowledge which are maximized for the inferior fall under the rubric of "personality and personal relations of superiors." In the eyes of the inferior, all relations between superiors and inferiors are *personal* relations and are defined in terms of the expectations and demands of the superior. The inferior, then, must structure his activities so as to please or manipulate the superior and meet his demands. He can do either only through an intimate knowledge of the superior.

Inferiors have many channels through which to seek the information they desire. Consider the case of the officer and the enlisted man. While he is on duty, whether in the office or in the field, the officer is surrounded by enlisted personnel. While he is off duty, the situation is only slightly different. In the officer's club there are enlisted waiters, bartenders, and janitors; in the officers' mess he is served and waited upon by enlisted men; if he lives in bachelor officer's quarters, enlisted orderlies clean his clothes, straighten his room, and shine his boots; if he is married and lives on the post, enlisted men care for his lawn, haul his trash, wash his windows, maintain his home, and perhaps, on occasion, mind his children. Only off the post is the officer removed from the immediate scrutiny of enlisted men and even there, because of his relative conspicuousness, he is in constant danger of observation.

If the superior-inferior relationship only among officers or only among enlisted ranks is considered, the observation of superiors by inferiors is even more continuous, for within these groupings the gap between the castes—which does at least prevent some observation—is removed. Few places where colonels may go may not also harbor lieutenants, and few places that welcome sergeants will exclude a private.

A possible exception to these observations is the general, whose position is so high that no association with a lesser rank can compromise it; and thus a general may borrow cigarettes from the private who drives his car and lend them in return, swap stories with his sergeant-orderly, and perhaps when they are in the field together and alone, give him a drink from the bottle in his bag. It is worthy of note, however, that within the ranks of general the old superior-inferior relations reassert themselves. During World War II there was a junior generals' mess at Supreme Headquarters in London, so that brigadier and major generals would not be uneasy while at meals in the company of their three-, four-, and five-star colleagues.

The only restrictions on this scrutiny of superiors by inferiors, and those that cause imperfections in the inferiors' knowledge, are imposed by military etiquette and by peer-group pressures. Even as one sergeant is reluctant to talk about another to an officer, so one officer is reluctant to talk about another to a sergeant, and few members of a peer group reveal its workings to a nonmember.

To put information relations into terms of concrete situations: Officers may and do discuss inferiors, especially with reference to their capabilities. Officers of equal or nearly equal ranks also discuss those of higher ranks to whom they are inferior, and in this context the subject of their conversation probably is the personality and personal relations of the superiors. An officer may discuss a corporal or a private with a sergeant, for the status of the subject of their conversation, being inferior to that of both of them, puts them both into the same superior class with reference to him. But the officer seldom discusses other officers of equal rank with a sergeant, although the lieutenant and the sergeant may gossip about the general because the vast difference in status between him and them puts them together into the same inferior status with respect to him.

The American Mental Hospital

It has been a working rule of the anthropologist in the field that the activities or objects or ideas to which a people devote conspicuous time and effort are likely to be those of greatest importance—and sometimes consequence— to them. By this criterion the mental health of their fellows and the institutions for the care and treatment of the mentally ill hold positions of little importance for the majority of the American public. Like the military establishment, the mental hospital is a product of its own history, traditions, and culture and of its place in the history, traditions, and culture of the society in which it exists. As a staff psychiatrist at the Menninger Clinic put it:[8]

Against continual deficits of staff and material, and against occasional instances of indifference, neglect, or outright abuse, progress has been made from time to time; but the uneasy feeling exists that reform and regression in mental hospital affairs are inseparable processes. The cycle has repeated itself too often to be fortuitous. The sequence of exposé, reform, progress, indifference, apathy, and decline has been repeated with variations in dozens of states of the Union in the past twenty years. . . .

The fact that reform somehow has never quite satisfied acknowledged standards of either quality or quantity of care has generally been explained as due to the fact that the patient load placed upon us grows faster than our available resources. Occasionally, political interference is an obvious explanation for the failure of the hospital program. The "unfair" competition offered by the financial rewards of private practice or of industry is frequently offered as the reason why clinicians are not attracted to work in state hospitals. Available public funds are often exhausted by educational and highway projects. These explanations have the common virtue that they absolve individual citizens, professional groups, and the general public of responsibility for conditions as they are. They make the task which confronts us so formidable that no one expects us to accomplish it. In a way these explanations help to make heroes of those who dare to do even a little in the face of unreasonable odds.

A sociological analysis of the operation of the American state mental hospital has explored this problem by detailing

[8] By permission from Alfred P. Bay, M.D., "Foreword" to *Human Problems of a State Mental Hospital* by Ivan C. Belknap, pp. vii-viii. Copyright © 1956, McGraw-Hill Book Company, Inc. The remainder of this section follows Belknap's analysis.

the mechanisms through which public indifference to the problems of mental illness is translated into abuses in, and the general medical failure of, the mental hospital. As in the university and the military establishment, these mechanisms appear in the form of discordant institutional functions and sets of traditional procedures which deny the fulfillment of those functions. The situation in "South State" is typical.

DISCORDANT INSTITUTIONAL FUNCTIONS

A crushing burden is imposed on the mental hospital system of "South State" by the definition of its functions and responsibilities contained in the laws establishing it:[9]

Perhaps the most important point about the South State law governing the state hospitals is the basic view set forth in the South State constitution that the main purpose of hospitalization is to protect persons and property from the consequence of irrational acts. While other reasons may be recognized for temporary commitments to the South State hospitals, the only reason for which permanent or "indefinite" commitment is justified constitutionally is that the patient is in need of "restraint." Nothing in this basic law specifies that the purpose of hospitalization is to cure the patient through treatment in the hospital and ultimately to discharge him to his home community. Moreover, the constitutional provision seems to carry the implication that the mental hospital is to be regarded as an agency of poor law, or general-assistance law, as can be seen from this phrasing of the provision:

"It shall be the duty of the Legislature to provide for the custody and maintenance of indigent lunatics, at the

[9] By permission from *Human Problems of a State Mental Hospital* by Ivan C. Belknap, pp. 32-34. Copyright © 1956, McGraw-Hill Book Company, Inc.

expense of the State, under such regulations and restrictions as the Legislature may prescribe. . . ."

In realistic terms the South State hospitals were actually being defined by state policy in a manner which made them in many respects the equivalent of the older county and city poor farms and homes.

The consequence of this definition of the hospital as an essentially custodial institution has made its function of psychiatric rehabilitation of patients difficult, if not impossible. Moreover, from the first their operations were defined as medical, and the institutions were filled with populations representing various kinds of medical problems. Institutional supervision was in the hands of physicians. From the point of view of the potentially redeemable mental patient, two worse decisions could hardly have been made.

In the first place, at the time the hospital was set up (mid nineteenth century) there was very little knowledge about the treatment of insanity, and, reacting to an earlier period of unwarranted optimism, most physicians sincerely did not believe that it could be successfully treated.

In the second place, much "insanity" *still* cannot be cured by conventional medical practice. The *physician* is not an appropriate agent for the treatment of much mental illness since it is not—at least in the *functional* disorders—"illness" at all.[10]

Thus the definition of the state institutions as *hospitals* and their functions as *custodial*, and the appointment of physicians as their administrative and supervisory personnel, created a situation where effective therapeutic treatment of the insane was practically impossible. This focus on *medicine* in the custodial *hospital* ignores the learned nature of much insanity and the creating and supportive aspects of the patients' normal environments.

[10] This comment about the physician is not intended to dispute the legitimate claims of the profession of psychiatry. Psychiatrists are doctors of medicine. However, beyond ascertaining that the patients' erratic behaviors are not organically caused (which not all of them do for themselves) they function as psychotherapists, and their conventional medical training is often irrelevant.

Further, due to the overcrowding of hospitals with the poor, the indigent ill, the senile aged, and similar populations, a protracted intimate therapeutic relationship between patient and psychiatrist becomes virtually impossible. Finally, as a consequence of the custodial definition of the institutions' functions, there are seldom sufficient funds to provide adequate treatment. The medical organization is adjusted to centralized custodial care. It provides adequate levels of health, nutrition, physical care and sanitation, but beyond this provision it is helpless to do anything further. This medical-custodial, hospital-centered organization, further, has created in its very nature the other problem which has made the state hospital largely incapable of performing effective rehabilitation. In organizing for "custody" within a "hospital-medical" system, a particular type of staff-and-line administrative organization had to be created, and this administrative organization of the state hospital also prevents it from curing its patients.

THE ADMINISTRATIVE ORGANIZATION AND ITS CONSEQUENCES

The administrative, clinical, and social structure of South State's hospital consists of two identifiable social systems. There is the "business system" concerned with running and maintaining the hospital as an institution. This includes the hospital superintendent, business manager, personnel section, accounting section, housekeeping section, physical plant and maintenance sections, food service, laundry, and various factories in which the inmates are employed. Alongside this "business" aspect of the hospital is its "clinical" aspect consisting of three classes of people: "medical" or "clinical" personnel, including physicians, nurses, social workers, psychologists, occupational and recreational therapists, psychiatrists, and other "professionals"; *attendants*, who are primarily charge attendants and ward attendants; and *patients*.

The business system of the hospital differs markedly

from the "clinical" system in several ways. Turnover is far lower for business than for clinical employees. Business employees are vertically mobile. Of those with supervisory posts, 86 per cent have risen from inferior positions, whereas, because of their "medical" status, promotion is impossible for clinical employees.

The grading of persons in the clinical system, and the professionally established barriers between them, are both the most typical and the most problematic features of the hospital's organization. They are the consequence of its dominantly custodial function and its organization along hospital-medical lines, and they determine what it can and cannot do for its patients. The three categories of clinical people—medical personnel, attendants, and patients—delineate vast differences in function and of prestige, and, being present both inside and outside the hospital, correspond to internal and external status systems as well. The three groups tend to be separated by differences in social origin, educational attainment, occupational history, social class, and age. For the patients, the fact of *being* patients introduces an unbridgeable gap betwen them and the other categories, while the social differences between the "medical" people and the attendants prevent any intimate—and sometimes any *effective* —communication. They often quite literally do not speak the same language. Needless to say, the views about mental illness held by the professional and the attendant are often not in accord. The consequent disorganization in the hospital introduces considerable discrepancy and often conflict between its formal and its informal organizations.

The Custodial Function of the Wards

In terms of the custodial purposes for which South State Hospital is organized, the informal organization of the establishment is reasonably efficient. Upon entry into the hospital the patient becomes a member of its lowest status level—the patient group. This status level is subdivided into three categories: (1) privileged and cooperative patients, (2) neutral and partially privileged patients, and, (3) dangerous, disturbed, or listless and therefore unprivileged patients. The new patient is placed in one of these groupings according to an initial diagnosis by a medical officer and by observation of his behavior and speech by attendants and other patients. The principal contact between the patient and the operational personnel of the hospital is with the six to eight attendants who have charge of his ward. The attendants are members of the status level next above the patients' in the hospital's social system and govern both the patient's position in the system and his relations to the physician. Because of the requirements of the custodial system, this control of the patient is predicated not upon his psychiatric condition or needs but upon his adjustment to the demands of the attendants' social system. The patient's first and most important job, therefore, is his adjustment to the expectations of his ward attendants. They are his primary contacts with the hospital structure and even mediate the few contacts he has with physicians, social workers, and therapists.

Medical and clinical personnel are isolated from patients by the nature of the hospital's table of organization and the social system which interposes the attendants between them. The attendant is supposed to act as an auxiliary aide in the treatment prescribed by medical and clinical personnel. In actual practice medical and clinical personnel are preoccupied with the clerical and supervisory tasks of running the organization and their contact with patients is brief and sporadic. The attendants, therefore, become the agents in direct and continuous charge of the patients. This consequence of the nature of the hospital and its social organization and legal responsibilities is probably inevitable. Because of its financial inadequacies, the hospital is understaffed and the shortage of staff is always most serious in the professional categories where there is a lively and superior outside market for the professional services. Because of its legislated responsibilities, the hospital is overcrowded and its staff, consequently, overworked. Partly because it is a state agency rather than a private one, the physicians have to spend at least 60 per cent of their time on administrative detail: paper work and correspondence, record-reading and analysis, attendance at staff meetings, medical duties of a nonpsychiatric nature (compounded by the great load of aged, senile, mentally deficient, and similar incongruous inmates), conferring with auxiliary personnel, and so on. Thus the doctor is under heavy executive responsibility and so to a lesser degree are other clinical people. The frustrations among clinical personnel caused by this situation and by their relatively low remuneration lead to excessive turnover, further complicating the duties of those who remain and shifting the responsibilities of patient care to the attendants. The ward physician is handicapped by the hospital's organization in carrying out his duties at almost every point in his relations with attendants.

The attendant social system is essential to the successful fulfillment of the custodial-maintenance functions, the most important of the hospital's responsibilities. Supervising, charge, and ward attendants form a part of a social system which controls ward routines and the flow to physicians of information about patients. Because of this control, attendants have a good deal to do with the diagnosis and treatment of patients, especially since the physicians' overload and high rate of turnover make them dependent upon the attendants for most of their information about patients. This is the core problem of the state-hospital system: the dependence of the physician upon the least-educated, least-trained, lowest-paid, and worst-treated employees of the hospital, who yet have the most to do with the day-to-day treatment of patients and the diagnosis of their symptoms. This intolerable situation makes the physician almost irrelevant as a therapeutic agent. The attendant is actually charged with the custody of most patients, must maintain order, sanitation, and organization in the ward, and bears the real responsibility for "handling" the patients and for undertaking what treatment is given. Since the hospital is chronically understaffed and overcrowded the only thing which it can realistically hope to accomplish is effective and reasonably humane custody of its charges. This, of course, is all that is required of it by law.

However, the rehabilitation of the "insane" is often possible through modern psychiatry. But psychiatry requires intimate, personal knowledge of the patient and his history on the part of the psychiatrist and in the state hospital this is impossible. What could be called the "psychiatry of the public institution" replaces it, and this is a practice devoted to the effective administrative management of a large institutional population. The modern American state hospital resembles the state prison more closely than it does the private psychiatric clinic, for the good reason that its problems and functions are essentially similar. Patients tend to be classified according to the amount of supervision they require rather than their psychiatric needs, with the consequence that a ward population often consists of a group whose behaviors are similar although the causes of them may be radically different. For example, agitated psychoneurotics, excited paranoids, schizophrenics, and manic-depressives in the manic phase are lumped together as "disturbed" and treated accordingly. Such mixing of patients is contrary to the logic of any psychiatry, and means further that little group therapy or concurrent programs of treatment of ward groups become possible.

We had been told (as we usually were with any problem we brought up) that the mixture of patients on the ward was the result of the hospital's chronic understaffing and lack of space. This answer explained overcrowding in the hospital generally, but it did not explain the mixture. In pursuing the question further we found that in nearly every case the patients in reasonably good mental condition always seemed to do the housekeeping work on their wards. They also cleaned up after the patients who soiled, and they bathed and dressed and toileted the patients who needed these services.

In due course of time it became clear that the mild mental cases on all the wards were part of a definite work system of patients who performed most of the work of the wards under the supervision of the attendants. This work group was maintained without regard for the logic of the two official classifications, because such a group was necessary in the operation of the wards for the hospital as a whole. Once we had this clue, it was easy to see that it was the admixture of definite proportions of lucid patients in most of the wards for work purposes which produced what at first had appeared as a rather chaotic mixture of patient types.

When we suggested this explanation for the mixture to our informants for verification, they admitted that it was true and told us at first that this arrangement of working patients on the wards is a practical necessity for ward management, since the population of the hospital is badly distended and personnel in poor supply. But as we became more familiar with the wards, we found that this was only a partial explanation of the arrangement. The use of patient labor is tied in with the ward status system, and has many purposes and functions which are not simply the result of overcrowding of patients and small attendant staff. On the wards it serves as much to focus a definite system of patient-management as it does to get physical work done. It is in this area of management that the hospital's informal or third classification system centers.

The organization of ward work defines a particular status for the attendant and a set of patients' working statuses underneath him; and these statuses in turn determine the position of all patients on the ward. The principle of this system, as we saw it, was that the ward attendant must give orders in the ward which will be obeyed. If his authority fails with the patients there are no further levels of authority until the ward physician is reached. For most people, one element in authority is symbolized by supervisory rather than servile activities, and for this reason, although his job specifications require it, the attendant cannot clean up after patients.

In developing at this point a supervisory role which is not formally defined in his job, the attendant also creates the third classification system of the hospital. This system had developed from far back in the hospital's history as a device

● 137

which supported the authority of the attendant through his ability to determine privileges for the patients in return for work in the hospital and for obedience. And the patients in the working groups serve the attendant in many ways that go beyond housekeeping. Some of them are lieutenants, spies, helpers with food service, and with minor therapy. As a group they appear to be essential in the present operation of the hospital.

It is this third classification system, necessary in the management of the ward, more than any other feature which produces the peculiar distribution of patients in our sample wards. A sufficient number of patients in the privileged, or working status, must be present to do ward housekeeping and provide the necessary authority pattern by which the attendant operates the ward. This is accomplished by assigning, if necessary, the needed proportions of the "right" sort of patients to wards which may be made up of badly deteriorated psychotic and senile individuals. The effect of this practice is, of course, that of altering the second, or institutional, classification scheme to conform to the requirements of ward organization set by the third system." [11]

This ward organization of patients and their social relations about the status and activities of the attendants has far-reaching consequences. The most serious of these is the attendant's ability to define therapeutic progress and actually to determine the patient's chances for treatment and discharge.

. . . further acquaintance with ward operation suggested that there were two main patterns of rather consistent adjustment between ward organization and physician classifications. One pattern of adjustment was in effect between the attendant system and those doctors who attempted strict use of the clinical frame of reference and categories, and those who were experimenting with different combinations of custodial and medical classifications. This first pattern consisted of a

[11] By permission from *Human Problems of a State Mental Hospital*, by Ivan C. Belknap, pp. 130-132, cited earlier.

tacit understanding among the attendants that the doctor was to be respectfully ignored whenever possible. The physicians' instructions were usually carried out to the letter but very seldom in spirit. The function of this attitude was that of insulating the operating work and authority system of the ward from authority which was random and unpredictable (or hostile, as is definitely the case with most trained psychiatrists) with regard to the principles of ward organization and ultimately with regard to the institutional classification itself.

A second pattern of adjustment between ward organization and the physicians' classifications was present when the physician employed a classification system which was in effect based on the ward social organization. These were the physicians who, in the opinion of the older attendants, "Actually knew what was going on, and had the right way to do things." In organizing their work, the physicians in this group define their patients in three layers:

1. The convalescent and hopeful patients who show improvement and potentiality for discharge by adjustment to the realities of ward life. This adjustment is manifested in orderly conduct, willingness to do ward housekeeping and hospital maintenance chores, and a generally cooperative attitude on the ward.

2. The potentially hopeful group of patients who show general tendencies toward adjustment to the ward, and are at least passively accommodated to hospital life.

3. The patients who have little prospect for improvement, who show little adjustment to the realities of ward life, who are uncooperative, often disturbed or excited, of little use in ward work, and sometimes dangerous to themselves or others.

In practice the attention and treatment of these physicians was concentrated on the first of these categories, but with the idea that the passage of time would enable many of the patients in the second group to rise into the first grade and thus receive attention. This classification represents largely an adjustment of medical treatment to the system employed by the attendants in organizing work and behavior on the ward. Each of these three layers is associated with a graded series of rewards and punishments in the attendants' social system, and there is little conflict and a great deal of cooperation when the attention and procedures of the physician in charge become part of this system.

The second pattern of adjustment is perhaps the most usual one among the older physicians and among those with generally more state hospital experience in South State Hospital and elsewhere. In terms of modern psychiatric conceptions, of course, the type of medical classification employed here restricts most of the physician's attention to the group which probably needs it least. And the logic of this distribution of the physician's attention clearly implies that for the most aggravated mental cases it is useless to employ the physicians at all. Only when the seriously ill patient—by a process in which he receives little personal assistance—gets well enough to move up into the top category does he receive much attention from the physician. And the judgment of his progress must evidently be left to the attendant until he arrives at the top group. . . . It is difficult to imagine a medical arrangement better calculated to strengthen and maintain the existing organization of patient-management by the ward attendants.[12]

Summary

This chapter discussed disorganization in large-scale organizations. The three kinds of organization considered—the university, the military establishment, and the mental hospital—often manage to operate efficiently, but social problems are "built into" their norms and practices. Disorganization within organizations is usually of the variety illustrated here: the production of social problems through the incorporation within the organization of incompatible or even contradictory practices and behavior expectations. These problems then dog

[12] By permission from *Human Problems of a State Mental Hospital*, by Ivan C. Belknap, pp. 142-144, cited earlier.

the organization and its members although only rarely are they so serious as to destroy it.

Both types of social disorganization, anomie and conflict, are found in large-scale organizations. Anomie occurs when members of the organization incorporate contradictory or incompatible norms into their expectations for their own behaviors with consequent frustration, uncertainty, and sometimes anguish. Conflict occurs when different groups within the organization incorporate divergent norms with regard to the values to be sought and the processes to be used to attain them. Thus there is conflict in the mental hospital about the hospital's true function, about what constitutes proper patient care, and about the appropriate roles for patient, attendant, and physician. Within the military establishment there is conflict between the regular and the reservist, between officers and enlisted men, about regulations and traditions, and about the appropriate role for the officer. These conflicts, in turn, may generate anomie among the persons subject to them.

Both types of disorganization are readily apparent in the university for it has institutionalized contradictory norms by simultaneously accepting the disciplinary and institutional orientations as appropriate expectations for the behavior of its members. The professor may suffer from anomie in attempting to decide which of several warring norms he must meet or even who and what to be. Since the penalty for a wrong choice may be his job, the stakes are high and his emotional tensions severe. Because of the "lawless" aspect of university organization there is frequent conflict over funds, power, and institutional ethics. The fact that few universities have constitutions or even comprehensive and specific rules for personnel transactions further exacerbates both anomie and conflict.

Large-scale organizations are only one class of organized social action, however, and in many cases their problems are the products of disorganization and anomie in the larger society. The large society, for example, makes numerous demands upon the university for entertainment of the population through athletics, for the education of the average product of the public secondary schools, for public services as well as services to several publics, for vocational training, for expert advice to government, business, and labor groups, for education of advanced scholars and scientists, and for pure research. The institutional requirements for meeting these varied demands are radically different and, in some cases, contradictory or conflicting. Hence the university perforce incorporates strains and tensions in its operation. Similar observations may be made of the military establishment and mental hospital.

Chapter V

THE DISORGANIZED SOCIETY

The preceding chapters have discussed various social problems of individuals, groups, and organizations. In a sense all of the problems considered may be said to be the consequence of disorganization in the society since they have been shown to consist in failures or ambiguities in the normative order by which people direct their lives. Yet in another sense it would be improper to speak of such events as alcoholism or juvenile delinquency as exemplifying "the disorganized society," for they exist only in parts of that society and affect only a relatively small number of its members.

In this chapter the discussion is concerned primarily with problems of the society itself. While the problems have obvious consequences for individuals, groups, and organizations, the normative disorders discussed are general throughout the United States and are not limited to segmental communities. In each of the three cases included—the status of women, technological change, and the ethics of industry—the problems are the consequences of historical and cultural phenomena and their effects in some way influence the lives of most Americans. In each case the problem is one of disparities or incompatibilities in the *mores* of the society itself.

The Confused Status of the American Woman

The subtitle of this section might well be "The Female Sex Is Here to Stay, but Where Is 'Here'?" That the American woman has to play a host of disparate roles has been amply documented.[1] Some of these inconsistencies, incongruities, or contradictions in expectations for her behavior are built into the situations in which she is now permitted to participate as a result of her emancipation in the past hundred years from a legally subordinate status. Obvious illustrations of such situations are the prejudices against, and restrictions on, female participation in politics (especially as political officeholders) and in many occupations in which men earn their livings. The folkways which bar women from equal participation in the academic profession (despite a severe current shortage of personnel) have often been remarked, and similar kinds of restrictions could easily be found in most occupations defined as "male" activities.

There are, of course, exclusively or predominantly "female" occupations: nursing, home economics, modeling, social welfare work, and hairdressing are examples. Even within many of these, however, the top positions are often held by men. The "great" hairdressers and beauticians, like "great" chefs, are males. And while there are few if any occupations from which women are excluded by law, there are many in which they either do not participate or in which their participation is relatively small and often limited to sex-allied specialties. There are female politicians and judges, for example, just as there are female police officers, but politics, the judiciary, and police work are still, for all practical purposes, male monopolies, as are the armed forces despite their female auxiliaries. Relative to the number of males in medicine the number of female physicians is small and they tend to specialize in pediatrics, obstetrics, and gynecology, just as female members of the military establishment are largely to be found in clerical and stenographic positions. Margaret Mead has

[1] For example see Robin Williams, *American Society* (New York: Alfred Knopf, 1952), especially Chapter 4, Sections 4 and 5; Talcott Parsons, "Age and Sex in the Social Structure of the United States," *American Sociological Review*, vii:5, October 1942; Ferdinand Lundberg, *Modern Woman: The Lost Sex* (New York: Harper and Brothers, 1947), Clifford Kirkpatrick, "The Measurement of Ethical Inconsistency in Marriage," *International Journal of Ethics*, xlvi, 1936; Margaret Mead, *Male and Female* (New York: William Morrow and Company, 1949), Part IV; Philip Wylie, *Generation of Vipers* (New York: Rinehart and Company, 1955); and a host of articles and essays in the popular press and "women's" magazines.

pointed out the dilemma of the employed American woman in poignant detail:[2]

The sister in America has a very special role in the life of the American boy, geared as he is to succeed on a scale in which he is measured by his age and size against others of like age and size, and rewarded by women rather than by men. The sister becomes a double rival as she grows faster than he, does her lessons more dutifully, gets into fewer scrapes, learns the woman-taught lessons more easily. Characteristically, the sister in America is the big sister, whose side the parents always take, who is so slick she always wins, who gets away with murder—that is, gets the same rewards with less effort—and the day-dream sister is the little sister, over whom one can win without effort. The habit of American mothers of egging their children on by invidious or challenging comparisons is at its most aggravating in the case of sister, girl-cousin, girl next door. The boy is taught both that he ought to be able to beat her record, as he is a boy, and that it is fair to compare their achievements on the same scale at the same age because they both ride bicycles or sleep alone on the third floor or are in the fast-moving section of the fourth grade. They are treated as alike whenever it suits the rest of the world and as unlike whenever that provides a better goad. If a boy cries, he is scolded more than a girl who doesn't cry; when she outstrips him, he is told that it is even worse than if he had been outstripped by a boy and yet she may be almost twice his size and he has also been told not to hit her because she is a girl. Side by side they sit in the nursery to be compared on table-manners, side by side in school to be compared on neatness and punctuality as well as reading and writing and arithmetic. She sits and challenges him and beats him at least half the time and often more than half, until high school provides the blessed relief of science and shop, where girls aren't encouraged to succeed any longer. And as he sits and is beaten —at least half the time—he learns both that girls can do

[2] From *Male and Female*, by Margaret Mead, pp. 313-324. Copyright 1949 by Margaret Mead. By permission of William Morrow and Company, Inc., and Margaret Mead.

most of the things boys can do for which rewards are meted out and that it is intolerable that they should, because it has been made humiliating.

This is expressed in later life in the relatively high accessibility of most occupations to women, but also in the bitter fight that is put up, even in those fields where women are the best trained, as in some government services, against giving women jobs that carry high salaries or administrative powers over people—the two most usual ways in which men demonstrate their success. Many societies have educated their male children on the simple device of teaching them not to be women, but there is an inevitable loss in such an education for it teaches a man to fear that he will lose what he has and to be forever haunted by this fear. But when, in addition to learning that at all costs he must not be a girl, he is continually forced to compete with girls at the very age when girls mature faster than boys, and on women-set tasks to which girls take more easily, a sharper ambivalence is established. American men have to use at least part of their sense of masculine self-esteem as men on beating women, in terms of money and status. And American women agree with them and tend to despise a man who is outdistanced by a woman. When American women do rise to positions of power and status, they have great difficulty in treating their male subordinates with any decent sensitivity—for aren't they failures to be there?—and shrink with horror from making more money than their husbands to the extent that they wish to feel feminine, or throw their success in their husband's faces to the extent that their own cross-sexual competitiveness has been developed. So we end up with the contradictory picture of a society that appears to throw its doors wide open to women, but translates her every step toward success as having been damaging—to her own chances of marriage, and to the men whom she passes on the road. . . .

So there is built into the girl in America a conflict of another order. She too must do her lessons and obey her mother, or she will lose her mother's love, her teacher's approval, and the rewards that are accorded to the successful. She too likes bread generously spread with jam and an ice-box *that is always open. These are hers, almost for the asking. "For all little girls" reads the sign in a New York candy-shop window, "and for good little boys." Hers by natural right, but at what a price! If she learns the rules well, if she gets good marks, wins scholarships, gets the cub reporter's job, by so much she has done an unforgivable thing, in her own eyes and in the eyes of all of those around her. Each step forward in work as a successful American regardless of sex means a step back as a woman and also, inferentially, a step back imposed on some male. For maleness in America is not absolutely defined, it has to be kept and re-earned every day, and one essential element in the definition is beating women in every game that both sexes play, in every activity in which both sexes engage.*

To the extent that the little girl shows the attitude of Whittier's dead heroine (". . . I hate to go above you, . . . because, you see, I love you"), she rejects the dilemma. True, she may have to spell the word now, in the third grade, because failure is too bitter for her small, success-oriented soul to bear. But later she will shift the field and get out of the unfair competition, go away from the game of loaded dice and be a success in a different field, as a wife and mother. The desperate need for success remains; it is not as strong as for the boy, because for the girl success is demanded only as it is demanded of all human beings, and not with the threat that if she does not succeed she will not be regarded as a true female. Boys are unsexed by failure; girls, if they are also pretty, may be more desirable if they need a male Galahad to help them with their lessons. But this is becoming steadily less true. Subtly the demand for the same kind of character structure for women and for men is spreading throughout the country.

Although gainful employment of women is still subject to cultural lags and discontinuities, even despite the fact that the American labor force is 33.5 per cent female (59 per cent of whom are married), the major problem of female status in the contemporary United States has not to do with being employed but with being *married*. In the United States 88 per cent of all women marry at least once. And it is exactly in this status of "wife" or "wife and mother" (for the *expectation* of motherhood, at least, is culturally explicit in the marriage relation), that women today are, if not lost, at least foundering because the rights, duties, and obligations of this key female status are badly tangled and confused.

While educators have long noted that the American school system tends to train women to be men, it was thought-provoking to the writer to discover that a poll of undergraduate sociology majors in his department showed that only 5 per cent of the women students expected to be housewives: the significance of this finding lies in the fact that the question was framed in terms of *expectations,* not aspirations. No question was asked the girls concerning their expectation of marrying, but census data justify the assumption that most would expect to do so. Assuming the truth of the latter observation the girls' failure to expect to fill housewifely roles can, therefore, be interpreted as an evidence of unrealism suggesting considerable confusion about the roles attaching to female status.

The proposition does not have to rest solely on a poll of a hundred or so undergraduates at a single university; a perusal of even a small sample of the mass media would be sufficient to convince that on the secondary and impersonal levels, at least, the United States may be training women to be wives but hardly housewives. The heroines of magazine serials and magazine and television advertisements are uniformly single or young-marrieds of the upper income brackets, and, barring only advertisements for cleansing agents guaranteed to "lighten the drudgery of housework," there is seldom a hint of dirty diapers and unending processions of soiled dishes and linen, sinks and toilet bowls to be scrubbed, and the eventual agony of deciding—for ten thousand nights—what to cook for dinner and then cooking it. Yet these, and a multiplicity of similar tasks, *are* the housewives' jobs, and are the jobs that most women perform for most of their lives. It seems significant that the tasks are habitually referred to as chores and drudgery and that, in middle-class circles, the woman who answers the question, "And what do you do?" by saying "I am just a housewife," does so defensively. This defensiveness may be especially common in "intellectual" groups such as university faculties, where wives sometimes feel compelled to go to school, join social causes, or remain politically aware and active, but it is by no means restricted to them. The urban or suburban middle-class housewife who enjoys her home and family and does not *want* to be a committee chairman for the Parent-Teacher Association, or canvass for the Heart Fund, or belong to the League of Women Voters, is all too often characterized by her peers as refusing to accept the civic responsibilities of female status.[3]

This devaluation of the housewife is a relatively new thing in American life. It is probably related to the Feminist Movement of the last century which resulted in woman suffrage in this one, but is more specifically symptomatic of the diversity of roles available to married women and the conflicts which overlaps in these roles can entail. Kirkpatrick has described the main role configurations offered wives as follows:[4]

Cultural roles for women are containers into which plastic human nature is poured. . . . We shall distinguish between three roles provided in our society for the married woman, each role implying certain privileges and certain obligations.

The wife-and-mother role is the traditional role of the married woman. It implies as privileges security, the right to support, alimony in case of divorce, respect as a wife and mother, a certain amount of domestic authority, loyalty of

[3] In some social circles housewifery has even ceased to be a part of the woman's role. The newspaper piece quoted below describes a contest designed to select women "outstanding" in various areas of activity. Note that homemaking, child-rearing, cooking, and the like, are not even considered.

"Six Austin women will be named as 'outstanding' January 1 by the women's staff of the *American-Statesman*. They will really be named by the City of Austin, however, because Austinites will select them.

"Below is a ballot.

"Nominate the woman you think should be named 'outstanding' in each of these fields—clubwoman, hostess, gardener, volunteer service worker, arts, career."— Austin, Texas, *American*, December 8, 1960.

[4] From Clifford Kirkpatrick, *The Family as Process and Institution* (New York: The Ronald Press Co., 1955), pp. 163-164. Copyright © The Ronald Press, 1955, by permission of the author and publisher.

●   149

husband to the mother of his children, and sentimental grati-
tude from husband and children. Corresponding obligations
include bearing and rearing children, making a home, render-
ing domestic service, loyal subordination of self to the eco-
nomic interests of the husband, acceptance of a dependent
social and economic status, and tolerance of a limited range
of activity.

The companion role is essentially a leisure-class phenome-
non. The privileges pertaining to this role include pleasures
shared with the husband, a more romantic emotional response,
admiration, funds adequate for dress and recreation, leisure
for social and educational activity, and chivalrous attentions.
On the other hand, it implies as obligations the preservation
of beauty under the penalty of marital insecurity, the render-
ing of ego and erotic satisfaction to the husband, the cultiva-
tion of social contacts advantageous to him, the maintenance
of intellectual alertness, and the responsibility for exorcizing
the demon of boredom.

Finally, the partner role corresponds to a new emergent
definition of family relationships. The role entails the privilege
of economic independence, equal authority in regard to family
finances, acceptance as an equal, the exemption from one-
sided personal domestic service to the husband, equal voice
in determining the locality of residence, and equality in regard
to social and moral freedom. The obligational side of the
balance sheet would include the renouncing of alimony save
in the case of dependent children, an economic contribution
in proportion to earning ability, acceptance of equal responsi-
bility for the support of children, complete sharing of the
legal responsibilities of the family, willingness to dispense
with any appeal to chivalry, abrogation of special privileges in
regard to children, and equal responsibility to maintain the
family status by success in a career.

The existence of such widely different roles becomes
problematic when they overlap and when it is, therefore,
possible for an individual to be subjected to inconsistent or
contradictory expectations for behaviors in more than one
mutually exclusive role. Since there is a great deal of such

overlap in present American society, we should expect women to be subjected to frustrations and worries. One of their evident problems is that of choosing among roles. For every woman each of the three roles Kirkpatrick discusses has certain advantages and disadvantages, and each is honored and rewarded in some respects. A second problem, perhaps more frequent, annually sends cohorts of women to the psychiatrist, marriage counselor, or minister, or at the very least accounts for many quarrels between spouses: the frustration a woman suffers who plays one role, typically that of wife-and-mother, out of duty and habit, but who yearns to play another. This aspect of the situation is compounded by training women intellectually to be men. A third common problem is confusion in role expectations between spouses. The woman may wish to be a companion or a partner while her husband expects, and, therefore, treats her like, a wife-and-mother. This situation is apt to involve both people in psychological problems as well as behavior conflicts. Aware of her failure to meet her husband's expectations the woman feels guilt at her shortcomings and resentment toward him for defining them as such. The husband, aware of his wife's expectations, feels guilt for failing *them* and resents her for her resentment and for her failure to adhere to his expectations for her.

There is also the problem Kirkpatrick calls "ethical inconsistency," which results from an unfair distribution of role-privileges and obligations. Since a privilege for one spouse involves an obligation for the other, any disposition on the part of either to claim the privileges of more than one role without accepting the corresponding obligations creates marital injustice.[5]

There are structural problems involved in these roles as well. The *companion* role is an unstable one on which to base a marriage since it involves as its key values characteristics— beauty and sexual desirability—which are notably transitory. It is, further, essentially nonfamilistic. This role is similar to the one Parsons calls the "glamor girl," and is difficult to

[5] See Clifford Kirkpatrick, "The Measurement of Ethical Inconsistency in Marriage," *International Journal of Ethics*, xlvi (1936), pp. 447-448.

maintain with the obligations of child-rearing.[6] It is possible only to the rich or the childless.

The *wife-and-mother* role, of course, is that played by most women from time immemorial, but it is difficult for the American housewife to maintain in the face of the forces which tend to emphasize the cult of personality, marital equality, romantic love, free-choice-of-mate, and the small (two-child) family. Thus it would seem that contemporary social forces push the women toward acceptance of the third, or partner role, and current studies of the American family tend to confirm this view. Yet stresses mitigate against successful performance in this role as well. This marital form seems still to be emergent, so that custom and law have not yet taken account of it. Both husband and wife may agree in the definition of their roles as equal and independent, but society and law do not. The legal and social rules of the marriage relationship in the United States are patriarchal and the wife is defined as a dependent for whom the husband has responsibilities whether she and he like it or not. The second major stress involved with this role is that it seems tailored, essentially, for childless couples. A woman with small children *is* dependent to a great degree upon her husband in the usual family relationship and can afford independence only at considerable cost to herself. A third problem, which has not been fully explored, is that equality in decision-making often does not work. It is very well for husband and wife to *agree* how to spend their money or where to take their vacation— but what if they do not agree? In the case of true equality of decision and action the impasse is unresolvable save by unilateral capitulation or the interruption of the marriage relationship.

Technological Change—the Price of "Progress"

For some time there has been in the United States a cult or ideology of *progress*, a set of beliefs and attitudes

---

[6] See Talcott Parsons, "Age and Sex in the Social Structure of the United States," *American Sociological Review,* vii:5, October 1942, pp. 610-613.

which define a way of looking at life and interpreting the events of the world which is characteristically American. The component attitudes of this cult or ideology include optimism, an orientation to the future rather than to the past, a tendency to define change in positive terms, and a preference for new ideas and things over old ones. "Old-fashioned" and "obsolete" are invidious epithets in the United States and conversely Americans value "newness" in and for itself. Finally, and perhaps most important, there is faith that the future will be better than the present or the past. (How many Americans really believe—or ever even ask themselves if— their children or grandchildren will be *worse off* than themselves?)

Some of this cult of progress rests on realities in the American experience. In the very beginning the United States was a place of promise for great bodies of immigrants—the land where dreams might be fulfilled—where there was work or land for everyone, and where a man could make his own way and determine his eventual place in society by his own efforts, unhindered by humble origins or lack of inherited money or land. And chauvinism aside, for great numbers of the migrants and their children the promise *was* fulfilled. So the American Dream has, or had, a basis in fact. As Robin Williams notes, "Belief in progress involves acceptance of changes, the idea that changes are tending in a definite direction, and the belief that the direction is good." [7] The experience of their own history has convinced Americans that progress is not only possible but that progress has occurred and will continue.

During the nineteenth century the ideology of progress— by then firmly established in the American ethos—was adapted to the new complex of industry, commerce, and technology, and the term came more and more to be restricted to its technological-developmental applications. The only times the dogma that all technological-developmental change is "progress" is questioned today is when the negative consequences of a new technique or device become so overwhelm-

---

[7] Robin Williams, *American Society* (New York: Alfred A. Knopf, 1951), p. 406.

ingly evident that they cannot be ignored. Thus an occasional voice may be heard today asking whether the introduction of ever more powerful automobiles in ever increasing numbers is *really* a good thing when we have slaughtered and subjected to horrible multilation hundreds of thousands of our fellows with the cars we already have. The voices which query the progress in building ever more powerful thermonuclear weapons are more than occasional, and yet the answers to both questions seem already to have been given and accepted by the dominant society: change is progressive and will be permitted or even pushed headlong to its logical and presumably Utopian fulfillment.

Yet progress is not without its price. Some of this price —like the appalling vehicular carnage—is evident, but a great deal is less than obvious. The intricate contemporary association of "progress" with technological change often has immediate and drastic personal consequences for those who are most directly affected by it. The typical case is the worker thrown out of employment by the new machine or technique: "technological unemployment." Belief in progress is so profound, however, that the larger society may make little attempt to alleviate the personal suffering thus caused and does not normally question the belief that the introduction of greater productive efficiency is "progress" and, hence, good. Although this part of the price of progress has been exhaustively publicized, largely through the efforts of organized labor to reduce its human casualties, the effects of such "progressive" changes on whole social structures have been much less frequently studied. One such study is that of "Caliente," a community condemned to "death by dieselization." [8]

The case of Caliente was that of a whole community threatened with disintegration by technological change. It was a city that suffered the consequences of "technological unemployment" as a result of unquestioned technological progress. The problem it poses is that while it may have been possible

[8] From Fred W. Cottrell, "Death by Dieselization," *American Sociological Review*, 16:3, June 1951, pp. 358-365. Copyright 1951, The American Sociological Association, and used with the permission of the author and publisher.

for the buggy-whip manufacturer of 1915 to leave his shop in New England and journey to Detroit to seek employment as an upholsterer of automobiles in the industry that destroyed his livelihood, it is not possible for communities and social structures to so transplant themselves, nor is there a theoretical rationalization in the American ethos to which the members of communities so destroyed may cling for guidance.

Caliente was disrupted by the dieselization of the railroads, and since the railroads are among the oldest of industries organized for the maximum utilization of steam power, and the social structure of the railroad community was the consequence of long adaptation to a steam technology, the technical requirements of the new diesel technology had severe repercussions upon the city's social system. Caliente was a model railroad town, for it was located in the middle of the desert and the sole reason for its existence was the service of steam locomotives. As long as the railroad used steam, the town was essential to it; with the introduction of the diesel engine the town became obsolete. A glance at the details of the two technologies tells the story.

Caliente in the railroad vocabulary was a "division point." The location of such points is determined by the maximum useful distances a train can travel without requiring service of its rolling stock and change of crew. Under the technology of steam, the ideal distance between freight division points was about 150-200 miles and between passenger division points about 300 miles. Since Caliente was located roughly midway between two terminal points about 600 miles apart and with little else between them, it was a thriving one-industry town, secure in the knowledge that the services it provided were essential to *its* essential industry.

The general conversion of the American railroad industry from steam power to diesel power, however, changed Caliente's favorable utility to the railroad. The service technology of the diesel engine differs radically from that of the steam locomotive. The steam locomotive operates at only about 4 per cent efficiency and requires frequent but relatively crude adjustments and servicing. The diesel engine operates at about 35 per cent efficiency and stops far less frequently for fuel and water. It requires infrequent but highly skilled adjustment and servicing.

The great changeover from steam to diesel traction in peacetime would have taken a considerable time, for it could have been expected to have been slowed by the high capital costs of retooling locomotive works, the long period required to recapture the capital costs of existing locomotives, and the resistance of railroad workers themselves to the change. But the exigencies of World War II operated to effectively neutralize each of these factors. Locomotive works retooled during the war to produce marine engines and the cost of conversion was assumed by the government. Existing steam locomotives were worn out in great numbers by the demands of war traffic and the capital investment in them was recovered in high shipping charges and profits. Finally, war-created labor shortages were such that union resistance to the change was less powerful than it might otherwise have been and was, further, far less acceptable to the public than might have been the case in peacetime. Thus without the war the conversion to diesel traction might have transpired in twenty-five years but during the war was effectively completed in five, and better than a third of railroad division points in that period became obsolete.

Caliente was among them, for diesel-engine trains could easily make the 600-mile run between the two nearest terminal points without a stop. But this stark technological fact was not a part of the expectations and life views of the citizens of Caliente. Men had invested their savings in homes and businesses, many of which needed the profits or wages of a lifetime to acquire. The town was serviced by four churches and a 27-bed hospital. The school buildings were erected through the savings of the citizens in the form of bonds purchased from the city and which the city had to redeem with the taxes of the future.

These permanent evidences of the citizens' faith in their collective future, together with the typical social organizations of an American community—fraternal and service clubs, church groups, unions—all demonstrate that Caliente was a typical American town with a typical social life and subscribing to typical American codes. Nothing in what its citizens had learned about the regular and expected behaviors in their world in any way indicated to them that the stability and even existence of their social system was totally dependent upon a few elements of industrial technology. The destruction of the city's economic basis of existence by the announcement that the railroad was moving its division point, therefore, was utterly unforeseen. The town and its citizens—many of them bankrupted—were expected to accept their lot as the price of "progress." And in the American idiom the conversion unquestionably was progress, for the general public, as shippers and consumers, benefited from it through better and faster service and perhaps even reduced shipping charges. But for the town and large numbers of its citizens, conversion was catastrophic.

A few of the citizens, those railroad workers who moved to other division points at higher wages, may eventually have gained. Their pay was not adjusted to compensate them for their specific losses, however. The gains, thus, were to the public and to a handful of the citizens of Caliente and, of course, to the railroad. The losses and their bearers formed a longer list.

The railroad could figure its losses accurately: it owned 39 houses, a 116-room clubhouse, and a 12-room hotel at Caliente which became useless, plus some fixed and nonremovable equipment for servicing trains. These were torn down to save local taxes and entered as capital losses, which were deductible from the company's federal and state taxes. Since some of these "losses" were presumably recovered through the use of the more efficient engines, it is difficult to see that the railroad was severely hurt.

The city as a legal entity lost severely. The three-fifths of its tax income from railroad property was gone forever, along with the possibility of supporting the bonds for the tax-free schools and hospitals.

The severest personal losses were born by the railroad's "nonoperating" employees (railroad workers not members of train crews), since their seniority was honored only in the local shop and craft and was nontransferable. Many of them, further, had steam skills inapplicable to diesels. "Operating crews" also lost. Since their seniority extended over a division, the older crew members could move from Caliente to claim a job at another point, although many left their life savings behind them in the homes they could not sell. Younger men had to abandon their investment in railroad employment and find new occupations. Because diesel engines haul about three times more payload with only one-fourth the crew manpower of a steam locomotive, three-fourths of the train-crew members were out of jobs.

Bondholders lost—one cannot foreclose bonds issued by a ghost town, and, financially speaking, Caliente became a ghost town; for though some inhabitants remained there, taxes could not carry the overhead of bonds in addition to the operating expenses of the town.

The churches lost. As men left town the churches were unable to support their expenses and some closed.

Home owners lost. They either had to support themselves in town as best they could, or rent their homes to others who did. In either case their incomes dwindled from what they were at the times they built their homes. The dwellings were devalued. Many were lost through inability to keep up payments.

In summary, those who paid the losses most dearly were those who were, by accepted American standards, *most* moral and deserving: the hard-working and frugal pillars of the community. Those who had settled down to buy houses and raise children saw the values of their houses destroyed and their web of friendships in the neighborhoods disintegrate along with the neighborhoods themselves. (The childless were free to shake the dust of Caliente from their feet). Those who built and invested their own personalities into the community watched their works destroyed: their churches close, their clubs and associations and organizations disband and die. (The unaffiliated—those too wise or too selfish to involve themselves with community affairs—suffered no such disillusion.) The chain store could remove its sign, haul off its stock and equipment, and charge off its losses. The good citizens who assumed family and community responsibility had no such alternatives and were expected to accept this catastrophic inversion of their expectations as "normal," the price of progress, which, after all, almost always spells sacrifice for someone.

The traditional defense of the costs of progress is always that they are offset by benefits to "the society as a whole," but the citizens of Caliente could not understand why society as a whole should not help to bear them. And while the "laws of supply and demand," may be in some sense "natural ones," they could not believe that "free enterprise" required them to accept the market as the arbiter of their destiny. And perhaps most appalling of the misfortunes which befell them was the fact that, contrary to American ideology, the costs fell most severely upon just those who most "kept the rules": the foresighted, the cooperative, the industrious, and the godly.

Caliente is still on the map; it lives on as a legal entity for it takes time to exhaust the capital resources built into a community. A desert highway passes through the town and the trade of travelers on it provides a living for some through the restaurant and motel business, but Caliente is fast dying as a social community. Corporate property has been torn down or removed; some homes are still inhabited by pensioners, others have been moved away, and others, left empty, are becoming uninhabitable through disuse. The town will probably never be completely abandoned for it has water— a precious commodity in the desert—and the highway will always provide a living for some of its citizens. But the *community* of Caliente has already ceased to exist and its abandonment must be accounted part of the price of progress.

"What Was Good for Our Country . . ."
—the Ethics of Industry

That "the business of America is business" does not need elaboration by a President for it is apparent to the most casual foreign visitor that the United States is a vast commercial and industrial civilization. The commercial establishment therefore might be expected to represent and reflect the mainstream of American ideologies and culture and the main themes of the American character and society. There is an historical tendency to speak about "American ingenuity and enterprise," "American efficiency and know-how," and to point to the vast industrial establishment and the unending wealth it produces as evidences in gold and steel of these national characteristics.

But if the central institutions of a society may be expected to exhibit its most positive and dynamic characteristics, the same institutions should be examined for clues as to the nature of its negative aspects and latent ills. One such clue is offered by the quotation used to title this section. The remark was made by the late Charles Wilson, Director of General Motors Corporation, at the Senate hearings on the confirmation of his appointment as Secretary of Defense in President Dwight Eisenhower's Cabinet. The context was as follows:

Senator Hendrickson: *Mr. Wilson, you have told the committee, I think more than once this morning, that you see no area of conflict between your interest in the General Motors Corporation or the other companies, as a stockholder, and the position you are about to assume.*

Mr. Wilson: *Yes, sir.*

Senator Hendrickson: *Well, now, I am interested to know whether if a situation did arise where you had to make a decision which was extremely adverse to the interests of your stock and General Motors Corporation or any of these other companies, or extremely adverse to the company, in the interests of the United States Government, could you make that decision?*

Mr. Wilson: *Yes, sir; I could. I cannot conceive of one because for years I thought what was good for our country was good for General Motors, and vice versa. The difference did not exist.*

Our company is too big. It goes with the welfare of the country. Our contribution to the Nation is quite considerable.

I happen to know that toward the end of the war—I was

coming back from Washington to New York on the train, and I happened to see the total of our country's lend-lease to Russia, and I was familiar with what we had done in the production of military goods in the war and I thought to my-self, "My goodness, if the Russians had a General Motors in addition to what they have, they would not have needed any lend-lease," so I have no trouble—I will have no trouble over it, and if I did start to get into trouble I would put it up to the President to make the decision on that one. I cannot conceive of what it would be.

Senator Hendrickson: *Well, frankly, I cannot either at the moment, but we never know what is in store for us.*[9]

The inability of either Mr. Wilson or Senator Hendrickson to conceive of a situation in which Wilson's interests as head of General Motors might conflict with the best interests of a national government which spends billions annually to purchase goods some of which are produced by General Motors might seem peculiar to many people—especially in the later light of recent court decisions against some of the nation's giant electrical manufacturers for price-fixing and bid-rigging which had the effect of defrauding the government. But the institutional egocentrism of Wilson's outlook is not peculiar to General Motors or to "Engine Charlie" Wilson. The consequences of similar corporate viewpoints have created serious social problems in the United States.

It has often been noted by social scientists and journalists that organizations, like societies, know no morality because, unlike men, they are immortal as well as incapable of pain or fear or sympathy. But whether, as this remark implies, human ethical systems are the consequences of man's mortality and empathy, the history of American corporate structures and relations shows a frequent lack of ethics in their dealings with the public. Because the United States is a business and in-dustrial society, this fact is an evidence of social disorganiza-tion, for there is a well-articulated ideology of social justice

[9] Hearings before the Committee on Armed Services, United States Senate, Eighty-third Congress, First Session on Nominee Designates, January 15-16, 1953.

● 161

calling for honesty and integrity in the humane use of human beings.

Perhaps the best known documentation of corporate irresponsibility is E. H. Sutherland's *White Collar Crime* in which the criminal records of 70 major American corporations are examined with regard to patent, trade-mark, and copyright infringements, restraint of trade, rebates, misrepresentation in advertising, unfair labor practices, financial manipulations, and war crimes. In their histories, these 70 corporations by 1949 had 980 court or commission decisions rendered against them for violations of laws or regulations of the types listed, and roughly 60 per cent of them had been convicted of criminal offenses an average of four times each. Of the 70, 30 were either illegal in origin or began illegal operations immediately upon their establishment, and 8 others were probably illegal in origin or initial policies.[10] Had they been human beings instead of corporations, most of the seventy would probably be serving long prison terms as "habitual criminals."

Sutherland shows that the corporations he studied have committed crimes against consumers, competitors, stockholders, investors, inventors, employees, and the government. These crimes were not rare and accidental violations of technical regulations but were deliberate, repetitive, and consistent. He concludes, in fact, that our corporations are "ideal delinquents":

. . . *The criminality of the corporations, like that of professional thieves, is persistent.* . . . [*Of the 70, 97.1 per cent were recidivists—repeaters.*]

. . . *The illegal behavior is much more extensive than the prosecutions and complaints indicate.* [*Many violations are industry-wide.*]

. . . *The businessman who violates the laws which are designed to regulate business does not customarily lose status among his business associates.* [*The violation of a legal code is not necessarily the violation of a business code.*]

[10] E. H. Sutherland, *White Collar Crime* (New York: The Dryden Press, Inc., 1949), pp. 23-25.

. . . *Businessmen customarily feel and express contempt for law, for government, and for government personnel. [They restrict and impede the businessmen's behaviors.]* [11]

These are the points of greatest similarity which Sutherland finds between corporate businessmen and the professional criminal. The most significant point of difference is that the professional thief conceives of himself as a criminal and is so conceived by the public, whereas the businessman thinks of himself and is thought of as a respectable citizen.

Clearly many of the individual businessmen responsible for these outrages against the public would never steal at gunpoint or personally commit bodily harm. Why, then, do they consistently and repeatedly rob the public through monopolistic "kiting" of prices and for the sake of profit offer to an unsuspecting public products known to be inferior, shoddy, dangerous, and in extreme cases, poisonous or carcinogenic (cancer-causing)? [12]

The recent Delaney and Kefauver Committee hearings disclosed that collusion, persuasion, and perhaps outright bribery in connection with the merchandising of drugs and foods frequently go so far as to convert the government regulatory agencies such as the Food and Drug Administration and the Federal Trade Commission into propagandists for and sponsors of the commercial producers. The "ethical" drug industry is a case in point which has been recently publicized. [13]

The so-called "ethical" branch of the pharmaceutical industry produces drugs sold by prescription only. There are over one thousand such firms, but twenty of them account for nine-tenths of the $2 billion of annual sales, chiefly to druggists and wholesalers. Although it is the sick person who foots the bill, the target of drug promotion is the prescribing physician. This is a unique situation—the ultimate consumer, the patient, has no choice among products and no influence

---

[11] *Ibid.*, pp. 218-220.

[12] See William Longgood, *The Poisons in Your Food* (New York: Simon and Schuster), 1960.

[13] The following section is from, "The Strange Ethics of the Ethical Drug Industry," by Alek A. Rozental, *Harper's Magazine*, 220:1320, May 1960. Copyright © 1960 by Alek Rozental and used with his permission.

over their price and quality. The physician seldom knows the price of the drug he prescribes and in any event is unlikely to worry about cost if he is convinced that it is indicated. Drug advertisements carefully avoid any mention of price and the salesmen—known as detail men—who call on doctors gloss over this question. Pharmacists also tend to object if a doctor tells his patient the probable price of a prescription.

During the last decade, the traditional relationship between drugmaker and doctor has been reversed. Instead of supplying the drugs he wants, the industry now tries to tell him what he should want. This is done by the same promotion methods that sell deodorants. . . .

In the past there has been within the industry the kind of competition that leads to lower prices. For example, penicillin and streptomycin, the most truly wonderful drugs of the post-war era, could be produced by anyone who wanted to. They were not protected by patents and exclusive agreements, and their price fell precipitously a few years after their introduction. . . .

No such price drop has recurred as the drug firms exploited the successors to cortisone. . . .

Whatever the legal status of the matter, the prices of prednisone to the druggist have remained unchanged since 1956. When sold under a variety of trade names such as Delta or Meticorten, these steroids fetch a price considerably in excess of what they sell for as plain, generic prednisone. For example, the president of a large drug store chain told the Kefauver Committee that he bought prednisone from a reputable maker at one-tenth the price charged by the signatories of the Schering Agreement. Unfortunately the price cutters can seldom crack the retail market and they have to sell cheaply to government hospitals where bidding is competitive. In that market the large drug firms compete by offering the same drug at a minute fraction of the price they charge the druggists. Thus, the president of Ciba recently admitted to the Kefauver Committee that it charges retailers $39.50 a thousand for a tranquilizer tablet it sells to the government for sixty cents a thousand. . . .

The drug industry's favorite defense of its high returns

is the fact that it spends more than three times as much on research, in proportion to sales, as does American industry as a whole. But in fact for every pharmaceutical dollar spent on research, four are spent on promotion and selling. Moreover, much of this research money goes into "development," which consists chiefly in devising new dosage forms and combinations of ingredients.

The drug makers continually strive for the impression that profits are merely a means of doing research that will benefit humanity. "A profit must be made," said a Lederle spokesman, "to pay for continuing research to develop new and better antibiotics." "We have made this growth," said Francis Brown of Schering, "on the basis of our dedication to a cause, the cause of health. . . ."

But much more frequently research is directed at commercial exploitation and undertaken reluctantly or not at all when the payoff appears distant or uncertain. For example, Dr. Theodore Klumpp of Winthrop, formerly a professor at Yale and an official of both the Federal Drug Administration and the American Medical Association, once pleaded, "Give us time and enough profits to do research." Yet when invited by the National Foundation to participate in the development of the Salk vaccine he declined, saying, "We felt it would be a socialized rat race." This premonition seems to have been unwarranted. When the Justice Department indicted the makers of the vaccine for criminal conspiracy and demanded to see their books in the pre-trial examination, the manufacturers opposed the request on the grounds that disclosure of their high profits might prejudice the jury. . . .

How is it that the ethical drug industry has not come into sharp conflict with the several agencies that are supposed to guard its integrity—the Food and Drug Administration, the Federal Trade Commission and the American Medical Association?

Certainly all of them must accept some blame for the lowering of standards. The Food and Drug Administration, to be sure, is primarily responsible for the safety and purity of drugs rather than their therapeutic merits. But even within these narrowly interpreted powers, the agency does not act

● 165

*soon enough or energetically enough. Seldom has it remon-
strated about preposterous claims which have evoked protests
in the medical journals. . . .*

The majority of the people working for FDA are honest
and conscientious but there are some curious exceptions. One
high official writes panegyrics in favor of dubious combinations and up to very recently was also the paid editor of two
medical journals of uncertain independence. Some of the
personnel of FDA enter the agency as a stepping-stone to a
more lucrative career with the drug industry and indeed there
is a disquieting movement of top officials back and forth between the industry and the FDA. . . .

What about the American Medical Association? It too
seems to have little interest in curbing the excesses of the drug
houses. Its publication, New and Non-Official Remedies, re-
views only a small fraction of drugs marketed every year and
does not generally consider combinations. Moreover, NNR
does not endorse any drugs, makes no efficacy and cost comparisons with competing remedies, couches its analysis in
highly technical language, and, in brief, is of little use to the
practicing physician.

The executives of the AMA are very sympathetic to the
problems of the drug industry. Said a former president of the
Association, "Both the medical profession and pharmacy must
shoulder one major public relations objective: to tell the
American people, over and over, that nearly all of today's
drugs, especially, the antibiotics, are bargains at any price."
This presumably applied to penicillin V which costs twenty-
five cents a tablet—twice as much as penicillin G which is
just as good. When, in following this advice, the manufacturers used techniques more appropriate to selling soap, as
Dr. Harry Dowling of the University of Illinois complained
in his now famous article, "Twixt the Cup and the Lip," the
editors of the Journal of AMA protested that "In a free enterprise system such as exists in the United States where there
is competition and a need for some return for shareholders,
one finds evidence of such selling whether it be the manufacturer of cars, appliances, clothing, or foods." I do not know
how much this attitude of the AMA stems from the fact that

half of its budget comes from ethical drug advertising. But I rather suspect that at least equally important is the fact that stern criticism of the drug makers carries the implication that not all doctors are well trained and that they occasionally are susceptible to trickery.

The electrical-company convictions referred to earlier are the most recent examples of lack of corporate ethics in American practice. In agreement with Sutherland's definition in *White Collar Crime*, the convicted criminals in this case were respected members of the business community and certainly not "criminals" in the sense that most people mean when they use that word. The social problem of this kind of criminality cannot be eliminated through better education for some depressed class of American citizens nor by psychiatric attention to disturbed personalities. The problem springs from the fabric of American society itself and from the expectations for behavior that Americans learn as a part of their normal socialization. This perspective is seen in the following editorial published at the time of the convictions of the electrical company executives.[14]

The organization man stands indicted in the eyes of the world.

This is the real indictment in the Philadelphia antitrust suit against 29 of the United States' finest electrical companies and 45 of their officers for price-fixing and bid-rigging.

Chief Judge J. Cullen Ganey of the United States District court observed, "I am convinced that in the great number of these defendants' cases, they were torn between conscience and an approved corporate policy, with the rewarding objectives of promotion, comfortable security and large salaries—in short the organization or the company man, the conformist, who goes along with his superiors and finds balm for his conscience in additional comforts and the security of his place in the corporate setup."

Judge Ganey also argued that he was "not at all unmind-

---

[14] Nate White, "Trend of the Economy: Indictment of the Organization Man," *Christian Science Monitor*, February 8, 1961. Reprinted by permission of the *Christian Science Monitor*, Boston, Mass.

ful that the real blame is to be laid at the doorstep of the corporate defendants and those who guide and direct their policy. While the Department of Justice has acknowledged that it was unable to uncover probative evidence which could secure a conviction beyond a reasonable doubt of those in the highest echelons of the corporations here involved, in a broader sense they bear a grave responsibility for the present situation, for one would be most naive indeed to believe that these violations of the law, so long persisted in, affecting so large a segment of the industry and finally, involving so many millions upon millions of dollars, were facts unknown to those responsible for the conduct of the corporation. . . ."

In reporting the case, Anthony Lewis of the New York Times wrote of the individual defendants, "They were middle-class men in Ivy League suits—typical businessmen in appearance, men who would never be taken for lawbreakers. Over and over their lawyers described them as pillars of their communities.

"Several were deacons or vestrymen of their churches. One was president of his local chamber of commerce, another a hospital board member, another chief fund raiser for the community chest, another a bank director, another director of the taxpayer's association, another an organizer of the local Little League."

The annual corporate sales covered by the indictments amounted to $1,750,000,000. The sales were made as sealed bids to federal, state, and municipal governments, as well as in connection with a wide variety of products sold to private utilities.

Fines imposed totaled $1,924,500.

Judge Ganey reasoned that the companies and individuals had "flagrantly mocked the image of that economic system of free enterprise which we profess to the country and destroyed the model which we offer today as a free world alternative to state control and eventual dictatorship. . . ."

Other matters are illustrated by this case, however. There is the problem of corporate bigness. This is no day for big business to operate in small ways. It is big. It must get bigger.

It must operate in big ways. Its executives and employees are part of a system of bigness.

The government itself is the biggest of corporate structures.

While Americans are brought up through their primary and secondary schools, and in their summer camps, and college and university sports, on the idea of "team play," they nevertheless have been taught from their youth that honesty is the best policy, and that the "good guy" wins.

When they see evidence of shameless corruption among their sportsmen such as the basketball "fix" cases they turn somewhat sadly to new heroes. When they read of race "fixing" and even traffic-ticket "fixing" they get disturbed for a brief time. They loathe evidence of dishonesty in high places in government. The television quiz program scandals shocked the public.

Now, the most respected of their corporate idols and some of the respected executives of these idols stand convicted of this conspiracy.

Is this the penalty of bigness? Is it impossible to have big government without corruption? Big business without graft? Big television without payoffs? Big sports without a shabby underside?

The answer is, of course, that the fault is not in the bigness, the popularity, nor the public spotlight. The fault seems to be in a cultural accommodation to unprincipled action. . . .

Perhaps society itself has been indicted, along with the organization and the organization man. The fault may be nearer home than most of us like to admit.

Summary

This chapter has discussed social disorganization within the fabric of American society. In each of the social problems cited—the confused status of women, the human price of "progress," and corporate irresponsibility—the underlying disorganization is the consequence of conflicting and

●

contradictory norms for what constitutes acceptable behavior in the United States.

Value conflicts about roles for women produce anomie. Traditional norms for female behavior have been discarded to some extent and no similarly unified set of expectations has yet appeared to take their place. Many expectations either conflict with others or are unrealistic in that they do not reflect the possible or the probable. (The "companion" role, for example, essentially ignores the existence of children.) American women flounder among the incompatible or impossible demands made upon them and may be expected to continue floundering—and to pay the price in instability and unhappiness which anomie exacts—until more realistic and consistent norms develop.

The social costs of "progress" exemplified by the fate of Caliente are the consequences of both anomie and conflict. American society is anomic in that its value system is not entirely integrated and contains elements inconsistent with one another and has developed no adequate mechanisms for mediating situations where such norms conflict except where these are represented in law. Thus in Caliente, when the values of human dignity and the worth of civic endeavor were confronted with the consequences of the equally widely held value on technological innovation, no solution was possible but the destruction of one by the other and the assumption of the human costs by the individuals unfortunate enough to be caught in the clash. Conflict was present in that situation since the social groups involved, the community and the railroad company, while seeking consistent ends through internally agreed norms, were unable to share meanings and values to an extent which would have alleviated the disaster which befell the community.

Corporate irresponsibility is a similar case. It results both from anomie (in the absence of societal mechanisms for mediating inconsistent social values) and from conflict (in the presence of organized groups seeking agreed ends according to norms unshared with other groups and the public at large).

However, no normative system of an actual society is

entirely self-consistent. Some strains and discontinuities have been found in every real social system ever investigated, if for no other reason than that social change never ceases. Yet there appears to be a "strain toward consistency" in most societies. Their institutions are to some extent all "of a piece" in that they are mutually supporting and intricately inter-related.[15] American society, like any other, shares this tendency toward normative consistency. Yet American society may also represent more strains and discontinuities than are usually found in other social orders. The United States is still a young nation and its social system is chaotic and its culture hetero-geneous in the extreme. (Unlike the British Isles, for example, which have a 900-year history of relative cultural and ethnic homogeneity.) Many of the social problems detailed in these pages are the products of heterogeneity and may "work them-selves out" in time, perhaps to be replaced by others more current but just as pressing. In any case, none can be solved here.

What has been done in this book is to offer a way of thinking about social problems. Most social problems in the United States are not material but ideological. Before they may be solved the absence of stable norms or the conflict of ideas underlying them must be defined. Once the disparate norms involved have been identified, or the absence of norms discovered, men may rationally seek solutions. It seems un-likely that social change will ever be entirely susceptible to rational direction. In the act of solving specific problems as they occur, however, precedents are set, choices between com-peting values are made, new norms are created, and men move toward greater control over their own destinies.

[15] The concept of societal "strains toward consistency" was originally formulated by William Graham Sumner and is discussed in *Folkways* (Boston: Ginn and Company, 1906) pp. 5-6.

INDEX